Royalties from the sale of this book are being donated to Prairie Public Television for the support of local programming.

Copyright © 1983 by Boyd Christenson

Published by
PRAIRIE HOUSE, INC.
509 10th St. S.
Bismarck, N.D. 58501

All rights reserved, including the right to reproduce this book or portions thereof in any form or by any means, electronic or mechanical, including photocopying, recording, or by any information storage and retrieval system, without permission in writing from the publisher, except for a reviewer, who may quote brief passages in a review. All inquiries should be addressed to Prairie House, Inc., 509 10th St. S., Bismarck, N.D. 58501.

Printed in the U.S.A.

First edition 1983.

I.S.B.N. 0 - 911007 - 01 - 6 (softcover)
       0 - 911007 - 00 - 8 (hardcover)

Library of Congress Card Number 83-061982

Televised, copyrighted interviews originally appeared on Prairie Public Television, 1980 - 1983. The edited versions in this book are used with its permission. A portion of the proceeds of sale of this book are earmarked for PPTV's support.

Original videotapes of the interviews are maintained as part of the reference collection of the State Historical Society at the Heritage Center in Bismarck.

Editor:	Nancy Edmonds Hanson
Cover design:	David Pence
Photographs:	Prairie Public Television

Boyd Christenson
Interviews

Intimate portraits of North Dakota's best-known personalities...

**Louis L'Amour
Lawrence Welk
Milton Young
Harold Schafer
Roger Maris
Quentin Burdick
Dr. Anne Carlsen
Bobby Vee
Mike Morley
Jim Adelson
Lenus Carlson
Agnes Geelan
Fritz Scholder
Ida Prokop Lee
Cliff "Fido" Purpur**

PRAIRIE HOUSE

Table of Contents

Louis L'Amour   9
The world's most popular writer of western novels, who comes from Jamestown, talks about his colorful past, his struggle to make it as a writer, and all Americans' fascination with lore of the Old West.

Lawrence Welk   35
The Champagne Maestro shares memories of a youth practicing the accordion in the family barn at Strasburg, the Welk "musical family" of international television fame, and the music that's kept him young.

Milton Young   47
The late U.S. Senator from LaMoure, North Dakota, known throughout his Washington career as "Mr. Wheat" discusses his political campaigns and experiences during almost forty years serving his state in the nation's capital.

Harold Schafer   61
The Bismarck entrepreneur who built the Gold Seal Company into a multi-million dollar national concern reminisces about selling wax door to door, the dramatic success that followed, and the philosophies behind it.

Roger Maris   73
The Fargo native speaks of the Summer of 1961 when, as a New York Yankee, he made baseball history by breaking Babe Ruth's home run record. . .and the painful price he paid for one-upping an idol.

Quentin Burdick   87
The unpretentious U.S. Senator whose home is Fargo recalls the six losses that preceded his first elective win, as well as his views on the game of politics, as played here and in Washington, D.C.

Dr. Anne Carlsen 101
The woman who dedicated her life to the school for physically handicapped youngsters in Jamestown that now bears her name shares her insights on disabilities, human frailties and barriers of many kinds.

Bobby Vee 121
The Fargo teen-ager who became a national singing sensation in the early 1960s reflects, as he nears forty, on more than half a life spent on the road and the state of rock'n'roll music, then and now.

Mike Morley 137
The Minot golfing professional talks about life on the national golf tour, coping with the pressures of competitive play, perfecting a challenging sport that's also an art, and his own game of golf today and tomorrow.

Jim Adelson 151
North Dakota's most famous television sportscaster, the state's answer to Howard Cosell, directs his outspoken opinions toward his own career, his lifelong love of sports, and his off-screen life.

Lenus Carlson 165
The Metropolitan Opera baritone who calls Cleveland, North Dakota, "home" recalls his rise from guest spots on WDAY-TV's "Party Line" to life as a bright young rising star of international opera.

Agnes Geelan 175
The Hatton, North Dakota, octogenarian whose career includes half a dozen electoral "firsts" for North Dakota women talks about politics, writing and the maverick Bill Langer, whose life she's chronicled.

Fritz Scholder 187
The world-famous artist who grew up in Wahpeton, North Dakota, talks about his creative techniques, his influences and life in the pressure-cooker atmosphere of the international art world.

Ida Prokop Lee 197
From her home in Lidgerwood, North Dakota, artist Ida Prokop Lee began a career odyssey that has brought her "Prairie Pictures" to countless homes and captured North Dakota Indians in bronze.

Cliff "Fido" Purpur 209
The Grand Forks hockey pioneer reminisces about becoming the first American in professional hockey, creating the UND Fighting Sioux hockey team, and putting his sport on the North Dakota map.

Preface

What you're about to read is a book grown from interviews I've conducted over the past four years for "Boyd Christenson Interviews," my weekly program on Prairie Public Television. Each chapter here is based on a transcript of one of those televised conversations.

Most of the names you will recognize immediately — many of them members of North Dakota's Rough Rider Hall of Fame, and the majority still active in the fields in which they've made their mark.

Some are native North Dakotans. Others have adopted the state as their own. They may have lived here only briefly or spent their entire lives and careers in the state.

They come from all fields — entertainment, sports, business, politics, the arts, education and public service. One thing, however, every one of them has in common with the others: An interesting and sometimes inspiring story to tell.

There are many people I must acknowledge who made this effort possible.

* PPTV program director Dan Hart, who in 1980 suggested the idea for the series.

* PPTV cinematographers Greg Mattern, Dave and Linda Friend, Gary Goodrich and Michael Olsen, who directed many recording sessions in the field.

* Nancy Edmonds Hanson, who for years has urged me to write a book.

* And my wife Marlene, who first suggested a collection of some of my interviews in book form.

"People would really enjoy that," she told me. Let's hope she was right!

And thank you, too, to the special people in this book — a group of men and women who have deepened my own appreciation of the state that is my home.

Louis L'Amour

Louis L'Amour looks like one of the heroes of his best-selling western novels. His rugged good looks, broad shoulders and shock of unruly hair give him the appearance of an aging gunfighter. He reminds you of the guy you cheered for in the Saturday afternoon movies when you were a kid. And like the men he writes about, he's simple and straightforward.

L'Amour was born in Jamestown, North Dakota. No one is sure of the exact date, and he does not seem willing to volunteer the information. His family moved from there when he was a small boy, and at fifteen Louis began a life of rambling and working at a succession of odd jobs — as a circus roustabout, an extra hand on a tramp steamer, and in a brief but promising career as a professional boxer.

His spare hours were spent in small town libraries, where he learned the writing craft from the likes of Homer and Shakespeare.

L'Amour's artistic output is amazing! He authors at least three books a year and has more than eighty books to his credit, with the number of copies sold nearing one hundred fifty million around the world. Some three dozen have been made into feature films or television mini-series.

He may have outlines on his desk for three dozen more. While working on a story he often gets an idea for a new plot. He'll interrupt his writing to sketch the new outline and perhaps a couple of its characters. When the original story is finally completed, another or several more are waiting for his hand.

His research is meticulous. If L'Amour writes that a family traveling across the prairie was saved by an uncharted waterhole, the waterhole exists right where he said it was.

During visits to North Dakota in 1981 to receive an honorary doctorate from North Dakota State University and again in 1982 to speak to the C-400 Club at Concordia College, L'Amour traveled along the Missouri River to make notes on the geography of the land he still calls "home" — perhaps the setting for upcoming novels.

How do you explain your success, the fact that millions of readers love to read Louis L'Amour? What's your appeal?

I think primarily it's that I try to tell a good story, but also because I am writing about the West, which is very much a part of all America.

No matter where my American readers live, if they live in the West or not, they are at heart westerners. They feel that appeal, very definitely. They feel that in a sense I'm speaking for them, or at least saying the things that they like to hear.

You have made the statement, "There's a little cowboy in all of us."

There is — definitely!

The one word I found more than any other in reading discussions of your books was "meticulous"...the meticulous detail, the research that goes into them. For instance, if you say the covered wagons are moving across the plains of Colorado and found a well of drinkable water, that well is probably still there today — with drinkable water.

Definitely. At least, it was there at the time in which the book is set, because nowadays, with water demands of cities, some of the old wells have dried up. But you can still see where they were.

Now, you use as sources old journals, diaries...in fact you've been said to even read old newspapers used to paper walls. Have you really found material for a story in that way?

For not one but several stories. It was an old deserted cabin, and the family had used the newspapers for insulation, plastering them like wallpaper all over the walls. When I found them, I went in there and took them off layer by layer. Many of these papers went back to 1863. In one of them I stumbled on a passage that said Wyatt Earp had ridden into town last week. Wonderful stuff!

And that became a plot for a book?

Yes. Not that particular line, but others I found in those old papers have provided the material for a number of stories I have written.

In particular, I located a gunfighter that no one has written about or heard about. I am not going into detail about him yet, because he is my own special discovery. I used him as part of the background for the story **The Empty Land**.

You have also exploded some myths about the Old West. One that comes to mind is the stereotype of the gunfighters' walk down Main Street to see who would be the fastest to draw. Did that ever happen in the Old West?

Yes, that did happen, but not nearly as often as you hear about. It definitely happened. Bill Hickock, for example — it happened with him. There was a shoot-out in the street, though not a walk down it as such, between Bill Hickock and another chap. There were many others, too, but it wasn't a usual thing. Men just drew and fired wherever they happened to be. It was the accepted way of settling disputes.

See, a lot of people have forgotten that the era of the Old West was the end of what we call the Code Duello. From the beginning of time men have settled disputes with weapons. For a long time the outcome of trial by combat was considered the judgment of God. The man who won was the one favored by God to win. They moved from physical combat to settling disputes with swords, and then with pistols — in the West, very informally, the way they just settled matters.

You're around seventy years old — you say that "age is not important, but experience is," and you draw heavily on your experience. One of the favorites I've run across was your relationship you had with an eighty-one-year-old trapper, skinning out a bunch of cattle during a drought. Tell us that story and what ensued from that experience.

I was not quite sixteen years old, in love with Texas, and I was broke. All together, I had about two dollars in my pocket, and that was all.

I was standing with several other men there who were all looking for work, when suddenly a car pulled up into the center of the street — an old Model T Ford. A man leaned out of it, and he said, "I want a tough man to work, a strong man. He has to be willing to withstand the job."

He said, "It's the dirtiest, stinkingest job this man will ever have. I am paying two dollars a day and his meals. And if he wants to quit, he is going to have to walk back home, and it's seventy miles from here."

You got the job?

Yes. No one else wanted it. So I took it.

There had been a terrible drought. Around every windmill there were — oh, twenty-five, thirty-five head of cattle dead. Some of them had been dead for awhile.

Our job was to go out, skin them and save the hides if we could. We would make the cuts and pull the hides off with the Ford pickup.

Naturally, no one came close to us because the place smelled to high heaven, you know. But we would sit around the campfire at night and, after the first couple days, this old man would tell me about his experiences.

He had been captured by the Apaches when he was seven years old. They wiped out his whole family, but they had taken him because he was a tough kid and he'd fought them. They admired that. They took him and raised him, and he became, to all purposes, an Apache Indian. He had ridden on raids with Geronimo and other great leaders, fighting the soldiers, and he had scalped white people.

Sitting over the campfire there at night, he told me all kinds of things about tracking; later he taught me how to track for real in that difficult High Plains country.

He told about Indian customs, how they fought and how they lost the soldiers who were pursuing them out in the desert, things of that sort.

Information I got from him became the basis for **Hondo**, the book I called **Shalako**, the one called **The Lonely Man**, and others.

You were sixteen years old when you had this experience. When did you start to write about it?

I wanted to write ever since I was old enough to know anything. I wanted to tell stories. I was trying to write back then, or thinking about it. Whenever I got a chance I was trying to write something. But I didn't know enough about it.

You've drawn on other experiences in your background as well. You've had fifty or sixty professional fights. You worked in a circus and took care of elephants. And weren't you once shipwrecked somewhere?

Yes, in the West Indies.

I had fifty-nine professional fights. I lost five and scored thirty-one knock-outs. I was fighting in towns around the country, wherever I happened to be.

I started right here in this part of the country, at Jamestown. I used to work out with Billy Petrolle when he was first fighting.

Oh, the fellow they called the Fargo Express?

Yes, but before he became the Fargo Express. I knew him when he first met Jack Hurley, who became his manager, you know. I used to work out with Billy and his brother Pete in Jamestown at the YMCA. By the time I actually got into my first fight I had the equivalent of several years' ring experience.

You had a pretty successful career as a boxer. What prompted you to leave boxing?

I wanted to write. Also, boxing at the time wasn't paying very much.

I'm a heavyweight now, but then I was then a light heavyweight, which was a very tough division. I was big enough to hit hard but small enough to be very fast. There were a lot of good ones around.

Boxing has deteriorated a great deal over the years. There are not nearly as many good people in it as there used to be.

You told me you always wanted to write, even though you collected a lot of rejection slips early on — a couple hundred, as I recall.

At least that!

But you finally found the problem.

For many years I kept trying to write. I kept trying and trying; my stories kept coming back.

Finally I concluded that something I was doing was wrong. So I got a bunch of my favorite stories, both contemporary stories and classic stories, like O. Henry, Robert Louis Stevenson, and people like that, and I began to study them to find out what they were doing that I wasn't doing.

And I realized what every beginning writer should find out: that he is writing at least three paragraphs, or three pages, talking about his story before he begins to tell it. He should start telling the story instantly, right on the first page and the first line, and not deviate from it.

So you became more direct?

Yes, and I began selling.

That technique is really evident in **Comstock Lode**, *your latest book. In it, the family decides to come to America. You have them making the decision, diving for sunken treasure to finance the trip, and getting on the boat, all in the first dozen pages. So you still practice what you preach.*

Well, not long ago **Writer's Digest** uncovered some articles I had written thirty-five years ago on writing. I'd originally written them after I had worked out how to do this and had proved it by writing some short stories. They republished these articles and now have also used them in a book called the **Writer's Fiction Market** because I've certainly proved my thesis over the years.

Time Magazine *referred to you in 1980 as "the most famous obscure writer in America." How can someone author more than eighty books, have one hundred and fifty million copies in print, and be referred to as "obscure"? How did you react to that statement?*

I was amused by it. I am certainly not obscure to a lot of people.

That's marvelous in one way: I have friends everywhere I go now, and also people who want to help me. People send me old diaries and old maps and things like that that I can use. I have people writing me letters sharing bits of information that might be helpful to me. It's really wonderful!

You have said that many writers pamper themselves. How do you mean "pamper"?

Well, for example, they talk about writer's block. I don't believe there really is such a thing.

Writer's block is when you get to the point in a story where you can't seem to go on. You can't find your way to go. Or you perhaps want to start writing something but you can't find anything to write.

I think the answer is simply to start writing. Start writing about something. . .about anything. Describe some girl you saw on the street. Describe the meal you had last night.

The creative juices are just like the water in the faucet. You can stand and look at the faucet all day long and nothing is going to happen. You turn it on, and then you get the water.

You can look at that typewriter or look at that pen or a blank piece of paper all you want, but nothing is going to start to happen until you begin to write. Then it starts to come.

You have said that you can write anywhere — even sitting with the typewriter on your knees on Sunset Boulevard.

I did that once.

Did you really? Did you draw a crowd?

Yes — not too many, but some.

People Magazine got me to do it. They came out there to interview me and said, "How about this?" I'd made the statement years ago, and jokingly at that.

I said, "Sure." So we took a typewriter and a chair and went out there on Sunset Boulevard, and I really did it. They used it for a photograph.

You told me before we sat down today, Louis, that you have a couple of books in the works that will be set in part somewhere in North Dakota.

Yes, I do. "In part" is correct.

One of them will be about the steamboat traffic on the Missouri River. The other one is on the Sibley Expedition. That's where my great-grandfather, who was in the U.S. Army, was killed.

Your great-grandfather was scalped by the Sioux?

The Sioux. He was a lieutenent — Lt. Ambrose Friedman. He was leading the Northern Rangers and was with Sibley on that expedition, pursuing the Sioux out across Dakota after the Little Crow Massacre in Minnesota. He was killed in 1863.

How far along are you on those two particular books?

The research is all done except for a few things I want to see personally. But I haven't started the writing yet.

Do you really have thirty-four books in some shape or form on your desk right now?

I do, partly-done stories or ideas for others. If I don't stop and jot an idea down, I lose it. It slips away. So usually I will take the paper out of the typewriter and put another piece in and start the new story.

I do have thirty-four ideas for stories that I haven't finished or even started yet. Two are almost complete. I have a half dozen on which quite a bit of work has been done, and some in which a paragraph or a page or two has been done.

Do you ever find yourself backtracking — writing about a situation and then wondering, "Gee, I wonder if I did this back fifteen years, or if I had this guy in the same situation before"?

It might happen. I don't think it has. I don't think about that at all. Of course, there is bound to be some duplication in different situations anyway because it happens in real life.

You know, there's a point I would like to bring out that is kind of interesting. People always fuss a lot about plotting. For awhile there was even a group of people who thought a good book shouldn't have a plot at all.

But a plot is nothing more than a natural human situation that recurs again and again. One of the commonest plots, one that has been written about many, many times, is the conflict created by power and authority, a persecutor and a victim. We just saw two good examples of that in real life, in the hostage situation in Iran and the Jim Jones murder-suicides in Guyana. They're both that same plot exactly.

I can pick up any metropolitan newspaper and find every one of the twelve to eighteen major plots in the course of a week. They will all be there. They are just natural, universal human situations based on conflicts that happen over and over.

Do you ever worry about becoming predictable as an author?

Very much, very much.

That's the reason the story I have just finished, **Milo Talon**, has an ending that is going to surprise a lot of people. In **The Californios** I am going to introduce a entire new element in the story.

I am doing one that will be coming out soon called **The Haunted Mesa** or **The Lonesome Gods** which is completely out of left field. This is a very different type of story.

No, you have to keep doing new things. I have to for my own benefit as well as for the readers to keep my creative self functioning properly. I can't always keep working along the same line; I have to work in different areas, different lines.

I am soon going to do a trilogy, three books about an Indian, a Cheyenne. They'll take him from babyhood on through his entire life. He will see his first white man at the end of the first book.

*You mentioned **The Sacketts**, which became a TV mini-series — that it could keep you busy for the rest of your life.*

It could very easily. I have several stories already planned on that.

I am going to go back to the life of Tell Sackett, for example, who has been one of my favorite characters, and I am going to tell his Civil War experiences. I haven't told them before — several aspects of the Civil War that nobody has brought out.

One aspect is how it affected the mountain people, where Tell Sackett comes from. Although they were in the South, most of them were sympathetic to the North. They were Scotch-Irish and Welsh people.

They didn't own slaves; they simply weren't into slavery. Some of them fought for the South because they were loyal to their states. But a great many of them slipped out and came North over an underground railway like the slaves used — not the same one, but similar — to get out of the area and go north to join the Army.

In the Medora, North Dakota, area, there are still remnants of families who trace their roots back to the South at the beginning of the Civil War — probably the same type people we are talking about.

I am sure that's true. They very likely came for that reason.

Let's talk some more about this meticulous research you do. I've read that a professor at Stanford University assigns Louis L'Amour books to his geology class because, when you describe an area's outcropping and formations, you have been there and you have studied them all.

That's right. What he has done is take some graduate students and go check out my geology. They have written papers on it.

Also this same professor was asked what he would say if he was asked what geology was all about. He answered — and I think it was the highest compliment I have ever received — "You read the first chapter of Louis L'Amour's book, **The Empty Land.**" That is really high praise indeed!

He really did check me out in a number of cases, particularly a book called **Kid Rodelo**. Along with one or two others, it's set in an area of northern Mexico which is very interesting geologically.

When do you do this research?

It all started when I was traveling around, what I call "yondering."

You see, I worked around in mines and lumber camps and whatnot. When I was working in mines at a time when jobs were scarce and hard to find, I made a discovery — nearly every butcher and baker and everyone else in these little western towns had a mining claim way back in the boondocks someplace. They were hoping someday they would strike it rich. Maybe they were just using it for a vacation spot...

Well, to hold the mining claim you had to do one hundred dollars' worth of work on it each year. It's called assessment work. These fellows rarely wanted to do the physical labor. It was pick-and-shovel work, dynamite work. So I would come into a little western town and go around and visit people, ask them if they had any such work that they wanted done.

Usually they were glad to hire someone to do it for them. They would take me 'way back in the hills and leave me back there. After I had done their work, they'd come and pick me up.

I got into places that I could never have found on my own. I couldn't have found them with a search warrant! I learned a lot from that. Some of my stories are laid in places I saw at that time.

In one national review of one of your books, the critic said, "One thing I've learned from reading Louis L'Amour books is that when you are sitting around the campfire and the coffee pot is bubbling, the way you settle those grounds in the pot is, you pour cold water over the top."

Just a few drops of cold water.

You mentioned that in more than one book. I talked with a lady whose father is a big fan of yours. She said, "Oh, my grandfather did that for years, always put in a few drops of cold water to settle the grounds."

What are some other misconceptions that you've uncovered in your research that we still perpetuate today? For example, was the Indian as savage as we make him out to be?

Yes, he was — he was savage, but not all the time.

First, you have to realize that when you say "Indian," it's like saying "European." There was a very broad spectrum of behavior among Indians.

The Plains Indians, by and large, were warriors. Their whole prestige, their status in the tribe depended on how successful a warrior they were. So they were out to take scalps, count coups or whatnot. Also, stealing horses was a favorite outdoor sport. They were extremely good at it.

Another myth that you've exploded, though it continues in a lot of Grade B motion pictures and even other western stories, was that Indian women were very docile and stayed in the background — that they had very little do say about tribal policy. That's not necessarily true, is it?

Definitely untrue. Many had a great deal to say.

Sometimes it was said in the wigwam, the tepee or whatever you want to call it. Sometimes their influence was offstage, but at other times it was very much on stage.

Nancy Ward, for example, was called "the beloved woman of the Cherokees." She could interfere and stop a war. And she could interfere in executions of people, and did. In many cases her word was law. She had proved her bravery in a battle and she was very highly respected.

There were Indian women all through history who carried a great deal of weight.

What else have you learned about the Indians which most of us overlook?

The Indian was a great orator. I have a number of their orations taken down by an Army reporter on the spot, written down word for word. Those Indian orators will rank with Winston Churchill, Demosthenes, any of the great Greek or Roman orators. Marvelous!

The reason can be seen in Indian society. In the first place, the Indians had a very democratic society. Any Indian who was a warrior and had done something brave in battle could get up and speak in council. And they all did. They debated everything. Before they went on a war party, before they went into battle, it was all debated and discussed.

So when they went on a war party or hunting expedition, all the way back they were thinking about how they would tell the story.

This was the theatre for the Indians. They were anxious to hear those stories. The man who was telling the story could exaggerate a little bit. He couldn't lie, but he could make the bear a little bigger, or more of the buffalo.

All the way back, he was thinking about how he could express himself best. So consequently these men became very, very good at it. They were extremely good speakers with a great gift for picturesque language.

Would you have liked to have lived in the time that you write about?

Yes, in a way. But I would really rather live right now than any other time.

This is the best period. You have a better chance to live in an easy way. Even your very poor people now live better than they used to live. It was pretty rough — very rough — in some of those early days.

A woman wrote to you not long ago to ask, "Where are the men like the ones in your books these days?" How did you answer her?

I told her they were still around. You just have to keep looking for them.

She is quite an old lady, by the way. She lives up on Kodiak Island off the coast of Alaska. She was nearly eighty years old when she wrote that letter, and the day before she had killed a bear. She said that what she liked about my books were the men. She said you don't find men like them these days. She was quite a character.

How about authors that you like to read? You mentioned some who influenced your writing early on; do you ever have a chance to sit down and read for your own enjoyment now?

I read fiction very rarely, and then mostly on airplanes. I usually read stories of espionage and that sort of thing, which I am very interested in.

You know, I don't know why — but a lot of people are surprised when they find me reading anything but western material. But I read everything, right across the spectrum.

In my library of almost nine thousand books I have the history of the entire world, and I do mean the entire world. I have histories of India, histories of Afghanistan, histories of Iran, all the different parts of the world. And China — I have the two oldest histories of China that have been published.

I am fascinated by all of that. In one way or another it all comes into my stories. It enables me to see from a better prospective.

For example, in **The Ferguson Rifle**, the protagonist is Ronan Chantry, the university professor. He had lectured at the Sorbonne and at Heidelberg. Suddenly his wife is killed in a fire. He was very much in love with her and is very much upset. He wants to get away from everything familiar — all the memories — to escape the whole thing, for he is terribly depressed, so he goes west and joins a bunch of mountain men.

Well, now, I have an interesting situation there. Here is a man with a very thorough background in history. He can look at the Indian with different eyes than the average trapper or hunter can. He knows about the migrations of people in Asia; he can see their migration here and understand them better.

He also knows, and this is a very important story point, something about forest progression.

You must mean the story of the aspen grove. Tell us about it.

Well, this is a story of a treasure hidden in a cave under a white cliff. There were supposed to be aspen growing on the mountain above it. But the protagonist realizes that after all the years that have passed, the aspen grove wouldn't still be there. So all the others are searching for the treasure in the wrong places.

He understood that the aspen is a mother tree. While it is growing, the spruce starts growing up in its shelter. When the spruce gets big enough, the aspen dies out. . .and you have a spruce forest in its place.

So he found the treasure under the spruce forest and not the aspen.

That's right.

I wish we had much, much more time. Even another half hour wouldn't suffice, because we have just kind of scratched the surface. Louis, it's so nice to have you back home again.

And one final question, very briefly. . .how do you feel about honorary degrees like the one you're receiving at NDSU?

I think they are very nice to have, indeed!

Louis, enjoy your research back here in the home state, and we hope to read about whatever you have found in a new book down the line.

I think you will enjoy it.

Louis L'Amour and I had a second conversation some two years after our original chat. When we next met, his publisher, Bantam Books, had just released his latest novel **The Lonesome Gods** *and he was embarking on a new project, a major departure from the westerns with which his name is almost synonymous.*

Last time we talked, Louis, you were busy researching some geographic locations in North Dakota along the Missouri for the settings of several future books. How's that coming?

It's coming along pretty well, Boyd. I've been getting some very old maps of the Missouri River, some that go back before there was so much engineering present on it, so that I can really picture it as it was during the peroid I'll be writing about.

I'm going to back up here again to look around the Dog Den Butte area and a place called Prophet Mountain, along with several other places that I want to understand a little better.

This year, 1983, is a special one for you. It's the thirtieth anniversary of the publication of your very first book **Hondo**. *Of course,* **Hondo** *wasn't an overnight success, since you'd been doing some writing before that...but we'll get back to that in a minute.*

Hondo *was, naturally, a western novel, and you were soon recognized as an outstanding western author. But have you felt sometimes that you were trapped in the genre because of that first success?*

Sort of, Boyd, although I didn't mind the trap at all. I've enjoyed it; I've done a lot of my research in the West just for fun.

I learned a great deal when I was growing up here in North Dakota. When I left, I was already tuned in to it, and also tuned in to listening to older people talk. When I got down to Mexico and Arizona, I talked to the old gunfighters and outlaws and whatnot and had a chance to get so much firsthand from them.

But I never intended to write about all this at the time. I was pursuing the subject from pure interest.

When I first started writing, I was writing about the Far East where I'd traveled some, and about the sea and about sports. I did some boxing stories. Then suddenly I'd written a short story called "The Gift of Cochise," and **Hondo** came about as a novel based on that story and then a movie. . .and I was off and running.

Reviewers don't seem to review your work because, I've heard, it's an unwritten law that the big newspapers and magazines simply don't review westerns.

That's right, and it always amuses me a great deal. But that's the way it is.

I went into this field knowing I had two strikes on me. In the first place, westerns are regarded as second- or third-rate literature. And I started out in paperback books, which were treated in the same way; reviewers only write about books published in hard-cover.

I knew from the beginning that I had to overcome these things if I was going to ever be a big success. I've been working at that, and slowly but surely, I think I'm doing it.

You have eighty-four titles in print now, over one hundred fifty million copies sold. There have been movies and television mini-series based on your stories, and you're doing better than ever. I guess you can thumb you nose at those reviewers now, can't you?

I certainly can! But also, my books are being used by many schools and they're being quoted very liberally these days. Almost every week or so, I get a call from some magazine or some writer who wants to quote me or my work. **Readers Digest** has quoted me several times with things picked out of my stories.

I understand you receive more than five thousand pieces of mail every year. What do your fans have to say?

Mostly, they tell me they've read all my books. It frightens me a little bit. I wish some of them hadn't gone through them all so they'd have more to read!

They go on to comment on one book or another. Usually they find things they don't like about them or mention certain books that they dislike. It's funny: Every one of my books is someone's favorite, but I never can guess which one it is going to be for a certain letter-writer.

I get additional information from some of them. Some send me diaries, some old letters. Others ask for information on the genealogy of their families or maybe of a character with their family name I've mentioned in one of my stories.

They're very friendly and generally most complimentary, and we have a very good relationship through the mail.

The writing of Louis L'Amour early on was a far cry from the kind of writing you're doing today. You wrote some jingles in your early days, some fillers and poetry. Tell us about them.

Well, you see, I started out to write and had to make a living at it. I had no choice. I'd quite fighting professionally by that time, but in order to get along, I'd have to go out west where nobody knew me to fight once in awhile and come back with the money. Then I'd write until it ran out and I had to go out and hit somebody else.

I wrote everything I could write. I couldn't sell short stories in those days, so what could I write that would sell? I wrote fillers for magazines. I wrote two-line jokes. I wrote jingles, and I did pretty well. For four months back in the 1930s I averaged about one hundred twenty dollars a month, which wasn't too bad at that time — and I wouldn't have gotten a single check for more than twenty dollars. They'd be mostly for five dollars, maybe ten, sometimes two and a half. I use to write some nature stuff, poetry, for one magazine that paid a dollar and a half per poem, and I did quite a few of them for that price. I did anything I could do to make a buck.

You bummed around from the time you were fifteen until you published your first book. You've called it "yondering." I guess you could call that a tough kind of growing up. What kind of influence have those early years had on what you're doing now and the man you are today?

The first period of my childhood, while I was in Jamestown, was very nice. I loved it there. It was a beautiful little town.

After I left, though, I had some difficult times. I did some fighting down through the Southwest and worked at very many different kinds of jobs. They all sound kind of romantic when you talk about them now. They weren't romantic when I was there. They were simply jobs that were available at the moment, and, believe me — they were scarce. When you got a chance at one, you took it.

If somebody asked, "Can you do this?" you said yes right away. The only thing I ever failed at was bricklaying. I told them I could lay brick, though I'd never laid a brick in my whole life. I didn't make it, but I got two hours' work in before they fired me.

Do you still relive those tough years now, or are they past and forgotten?

I'm trying to recall them more these days because I've been asked by my family and my publisher to write an autobiography. So I'm attempting to recapture those memories. It's not so easy to sit there before your typewriter and recall those mean, ugly times. Yet I want to put myself back in that mood again to write just exactly what was happening to me at the time.

You recently told an interviewer that "adventure is another word for getting into trouble."

Yes, it is — nothing but that. It's trouble when you have it and wish you were out of it. It's only adventure when you tell about it afterwards.

You've had some adventures in Asia, too — Japan and China.

In Japan, I jumped ship because the food was so bad. After the ship was gone I had to make a living; I had only a few dollars in my pocket.

I was recruited to fight in a judo match. At that time, the Japanese were picking up Americans and Europeans off the docks, billing them as champions and pitting them against professional judo or karate fighters. . .and usually getting them killed.

Well, I'd done some fighting before they recruited me. The first time they got an inkling that something might not be quite right was when they came into the dressing room and I was taping my hands. Of course, there were no rules over there as far as that sort of thing was concerned, and I was taping them but good. They asked me then if I'd fought before and I said, "Oh, I've boxed around a little." By the time I left there, I'd won three fights against their judo experts.

Weren't you also involved in a war between warlords?

Yes, very briefly, in China. That was toward the end of the warlord era, and they were recruiting all sorts of soldiers of fortune, mostly Germans and English, with a few Frenchmen and Americans. I was recruited too.

What kinds of things did you do?

I ran a machine gun for awhile and taught others how to use one.

My brother had been a lieutenant in a National Guard machine gun company in Jamestown. He'd used one in World War I. I was too young at the time to belong, but I used to go out with him sometimes. He showed me how to dismantle the machine gun and put it together again; he'd brought one home so he could go over it a few times before he taught about it.

I taught that very briefly, and then got involved in the ring again and with horses from time to time.

You're now working on a trilogy that's located in those settings, if not exactly drawn from personal experience.

The first book is set in Europe and is called **The Walking Drum**. The second book will take place in India and the third in China, all in the twelfth century. And if I do say so myself, they're very exciting, swashbuckling stories.

Something in the first book is going to startle a few people who'll think it's just fiction. But it is not fiction. I tell of an underground passage in France that led some seventy kilometers across the countryside, big enough for a man and horse to ride through. It was built back somewhere between 400 and 700 A.D. No one seems to know about it now.

How did you find out about this?

I discovered it by accident, in a sense, during some other research.

Everywhere I go, I ask questions. I was staying in a little town not far from Paris where our troops were quartered. I'm always interested in things around me and wanted to get some background, so I asked about secret passages.

I was sent to a nearby castle that has some that everyone knows about. But there a fellow told me a very interesting story about the chapel, which was built in 550 A.D. His grandfather had been awakened years before by a priest in the middle of the night. The priest asked him to get his tools and come to the church, along with some other men he'd recruited. The church had apparently been built over a tunnel and its floor had caved in; the priest wanted it put back in shape for the next morning's service.

He didn't know whether the story was true or not, but it excited me. He told me the tunnel was supposed to have been built during a time when robber barons threatened the prosperous monks of the area. To avoid them, the monks built this underground tunnel clear across the country, so they could go about their travels without being seen or heard.

I investigated and found part of it. Down at Provence, which is at the end of the tunnel, they'll show you many underground passages that have been discovered. One of these is probably the opening to my tunnel — anyway, it is in my story.

How will your fans feel about this departure from the Louis L'Amour western set in the Wild West?

I don't know what they're going to think about it — but I'm curious to find out. I think some of them will go along with me. But others won't like it so well because they like my stories of America, particularly.

But this is also a kind of a break for me. It's like taking a vacation. I'm writing about something utterly different, and I can get to use a lot of material I won't ever have a chance to use otherwise.

Your writing three books a year seems to me a very ambitious schedule. Is there a particular reason why you keep yourself so busy?

Because I like to. I do better when I write fast and when I write all the time.

All writers have different rhythms. For example, Flaubert took seven years to write **Madame Bovary**. On the other hand, an equally great book, Stendahl's **La Chartreuse de Parme**, was written in seven weeks. And Noel Coward wrote **Private Lives** in four days.

It all depends on the individual, how he's feeling at the time, and that sort of thing. As for me, I just like to write.

You mentioned to me that you used to hang around bookstores, watching what people asked for, and learned from that the importance of keeping your name before the public. Is that also a reason you write so many books each year?

Very definitely it is. You see, people consider me a success now. I don't. I think I'm still on my way. But the point is that others consider me so, but don't stop to think of all the planning and the thinking that went into this beforehand.

Way back in the time when I didn't have a dime, when I was hanging around the bookstores without being able to buy, I was watching what people bought and thinking about their choices. I was studying the publishers' methods.

My plan, then, was preconceived. I knew what I was going to do and how I was going to do it. And I've done it.

Oscar Driscoll, who used to be publisher at Bantam Books, will tell you that it's worked out just the way for my books that I insisted it would. Saul David, who was my editor at Bantam, would tell you the same thing.

After I went to work with Bantam Books, I told them, "You're not putting out enough of my books." They said they didn't because they'd only be returned. (Unsold books are returned to publishers for full refunds by the bookstores.) I told them, "There aren't going to be any returns. Put them out there!"

It took me a couple of years to persuade them to put more books out on the stands. They finally decided to try it in two towns — El Paso and another that I forget. They were all gone the second day!

I had to teach them how to market the books based on what I'd learned by hanging around bookstores myself. Of course, they've taught me a lot of things since then. They've improved their methods a great deal and have generally done a terrific job for me. Bantam is a great publisher.

Speaking of improving methods, you've also mentioned that you feel your writing has improved down through the years. In what way, Louis?

It's improved in several ways. Now I have more leisure, for one thing — I can think more about what I write and not just do it to make a living. I think more carefully about what I'm doing, now that I have an established market and I know I'm selling.

I can take a little bit more time to think about the work and to add touches I couldn't before. I can be more philosophical. I can venture into different areas. I can write more like I want to write. I can also put myself into stories more easily.

My own interest in history and literature and art, and so on, was much more prevalent in the Old West than most people think, you know. Billy Hamilton, one of the early mountain men, tells in his diary about crossing the mountains and stopping at a pass. . .just to exchange books with another mountain man. He doesn't record, unhappily, what he exchanged. But he got back a one-volume edition of Shakespeare and Carlisle's **French Revolution**, which was a new book in those days.

This sort of interest was much more common in those days than people have come to believe today. I like to tell stories like that one — to present a genuine picture of life in the West as it was really lived.

How is it different to write when you're a cold, hungry young man compared to doing it thirty years later when there's food on the table and you're living comfortably in a nice home? What kind of effect does that change have on your finished product?

My finished product is better now. But the change has made a difference. I try to remember those days. Frankly, because of them, I'm very aware that no matter how successful I may be at the moment, right outside those walls is cold and hungry.

Things can turn bad in a minute. A change can affect anyone's life at any time. None of us really has it made, ever. We may think we do, but we don't. We're all walking on a ragged edge.

We've got the impression, in this society, that we ought to take it easier with age. When you're sixty-five, no matter what you're doing, you're supposed to sit back and suddenly not work anymore. And we wonder: Why does George Burns work so hard when he's almost ninety? Why is Bob Hope still at it, and why did Jack Benny keep working right up until the day he died?

So the logical question is this — why, Louis, do you work as hard as ever as you're nearing age seventy? Obviously you don't need the money. Why do it?

I work hard because I'm just beginning. I'm just getting going now, just reaching the point where I can say what I mean to say, write what I want to write.

I don't mean that there's been anything that's stopped me beyond my own lack of ability. But gradually that ability is increasing with experience.

My writing is gradually getting better. I think that ten years from now I'll be twice the writer I am today.

As I mentioned before, you're celebrating an anniversary this year, the thirtieth since **Hondo** *was released in 1953. That began life, as you've told us, as a short stroy. How do you go about expanding a short story into a full-length novel?*

"The Gift of Cochise" appeared in **Collier's Magazine**, and I thought that was the end of it. I got a call from Dick Carroll, who was at that time an editor at Fawcett Books. He said, "You know, you've got great characters in here. There's a novel in that, not just a short story. Take it and expand it, and we'll buy it."

So I did, and they did, and so did John Wayne, eventually, who bought it for a movie.

That first book was published by Fawcett but you're with Bantam now. What happened? How did Fawcett let Louis L'Amour slip through their fingers?

Fawcett only wanted to release one of my books per year, and I wanted to publish three. They kept saying, "No, the public won't buy more than one."

Well, I'd studied the thing very carefully, and I knew they'd buy more. . .and I wanted to sell more. So Saul David came out from Bantam Books in New York to see me in Los Angeles.

Now, Saul's a very capable fellow, a very brilliant man, and he also likes to go against the grain. If you tell him something can't be done, he wants to do it, and do it right now.

I told Saul what Fawcett had decided and he said, "Well, we'll do it."

The publisher, Oscar Driscoll, has told me himself that he was a little bit hesitant when Saul came back to New York and told him what he and I had agreed on. He said, "Okay, let's try it — but just two at first." We tried publishing two, and they sold, so then three, and they sold, too. Now they'd like to have twelve!

Didn't Fawcett try to entice you back into the fold some years later?

Yes, they offered me a pretty rich sum of money to come back. I told them, "No way."

*Your book titles read like music. . .***Hondo, Bendigo Shafter, The Californios***. Your heroes' names have lots of "O's" and rhythm. Is that by design?*

Yes, it is. I like to have names that can be remembered easily and spoken easily, and there's always something nice about a name with three to five syllables. I like them particularly well, though some of my titles are longer. I try to give them a musical sound.

All my books, for that matter, are written for their sound as well as their content. I want them to be read aloud as easily as read to yourself.

Your stories and travels certainly haven't been limited to the United States. Are there books in your future based on the history of our Canadian neighbors?

Certainly. I'm going to do the story of Louis Riel. I've been researching it for quite a long time, gathering material, and I'm going to write it very soon now.

Louis Riel is one of the great folk heroes of Canada and a very interesting figure of a man — much more dimensional than he's been presented so far. He's a fascinating character. I'm just sorry that Paul Muni is dead, because Paul Muni could have played him like no one else in the world. And he's the kind of man Muni would have loved to play.

Have there been collisions between the United States and Canada during the periods you've researched that could be the basis for other stories?

By and large, there have been few collisions between the United States and Canada over the years, though there was some friction over bootlegging and the fur trade along the border in Montana at one time.

At the time of Louis Riel's rebellion, some Americans were trying to acquire large sections of Canadian property. One of them was Stutsman, for whom Stutsman County was named. He was deeply involved in real estate manipulation, one of the things that caused Riel to start fighting on behalf of his people, the Metis.

Let's talk abouot your latest effort, published recently in hard-cover, entitled **The Lonesome Gods**. *What can readers expect from it?*

The Lonesome Gods is, first of all, an exciting book. It's set in southern California in the years 1840 to 1870, the period in which the Americans were taking it from the Mexicans. It has a lot about the desert, and there's some mysticism in it.

The lonesome gods are the gods worshipped by ancient people who lived and died long ago. The book's thesis is that when a god is not worshipped, he gets weaker and weaker and finally fades away.

My protagonist recognizes this of a lonesome god once worshipped by the Indians who are now gone. There are piles of stones where paths cross that are offerings to this god. His worshippers had a custom of picking up a stone and throwing it onto the pile as an offering to the god of the trail, an offering to lighten the load. My protagonist does that, and I always to that, too.

I think your fans will be interested to know that you're also working on an opera right now.

Yes, a musical and an opera both.

The musical is based on a story I wrote some time ago called "The Holiday at Canyon Gap." The opera is about the conquest of Mexico. It'll be called "Malinche," after the Indian mistress of Cortez — a very sad, beautiful and exciting story. The music is being done by a man from Utah who's written music for a number of operas produced in Bolivia, Brazil, Paraguay and Peru, but not in the United States.

Tom Selleck, the macho actor from network television, appeared in one of your works for CBS. I know he's one of your favorites and understand you're working together on a couple of scripts that might become movies.

Tom Selleck was in not one, but two of mine. He gives us credit for his discovery in "The Sacketts," where he played Orrin Sackett. He also played Mac Traven in "Shadow Riders," and wants to do another story of mine soon.

I have three stories presently on the verge of becoming movies: **Down the Long Hills** for one, because it's been optioned and they're working on the screenplay now, as well as **Conagher** and **The Quick and the Dead**.

What advice do you have for young writers who have a hot manuscript tucked under their mattresses or are working on one in their spare time?

The only advice is to write, and write as well as you possibly can. And read, so that you have your head full of something to write about, so that you know what's going on, and also so that you know what the others have done.

There was a great story by Kenneth Fowler in recent issue of **The Roundup**, the magazine of the Western Writers of America. He told about the time when he was an editor and was going through the "slush pit," as they call the pile of unsolicited manuscripts that pour in. They're mostly junk, but editors go through them hoping to find something special.

Suddenly he came across this battered, beat-up old manuscript and saw from the first line that the writer knew something about writing, so he went ahead and read it to the end. Later, he asked to have it purchased, and it was. He wrote, "Now you see that writer's name on books everywhere."

It was one of my stories.

It takes a strong constitution to survive in your field. What have you had, a couple hundred rejections in your day?

At least that. Probably more. You've got to be determined. I've often said of my kids that I'd rather have them determined than brilliant.

You have a son, Beau, who's following in your footsteps as a writer. Does he ever come to Dad for pointers?

He wants to write and direct movies, and has finished one and is working on another. He doesn't come to me for advice, though. He writes in his own way and wants to build his own career — be his own man.

He does want to use some of my stories for screenplays, however.

Don't you also have a daughter starting her career?

Angelique's an actress and singer — at least, she's starting to be. She was an extra in my picture "Shadow Riders." She got the job on her own.

My wife Kathy Adams was an actress when we met, and so was her mother Joan Meredith, who played in quite a few pictures in the old silent films.

Louis, we're looking forward to whatever comes next from your typewriter. It's fascinating that you still say your career is just beginning and that ten years from now you'll be an even better writer. What a marvelous attitude!

Well, that's the way I feel. I can definitely feel the improvement coming on.

One other thing I feel and I hope you'll remember, Boyd. Regardless of where I am, North Dakota is always home to me.

A short time after the interview with Louis L'Amour was aired on Prairie Public Television, I received a phone call from a nurse at a hospital in a small Minnesota community. She told me that one of her patients, a man suffering from cancer, was an avid L'Amour fan and had read all of the author's books.

"Would it be possible for Mr. L'Amour to make contact with his fan out here?" she asked me.

I called Louis at his home in California, and we arranged a time for a telephone visit. The two men talked for a long time.

Later the nurse told me about her patient, "It was quite a day for him. He was so excited he put on a clean gown and combed his hair for the call."

Lawrence Welk

My conversation with Lawrence Welk was almost interrupted by the eruption of Mt. St. Helens, the volcano in Washington.

Let me explain.

Each year Welk returns to North Dakota to play golf with a group of his friends. We thought it might be interesting to follow the maestro for a few holes on the golf course at Apple Creek Country Club in Bismarck, and then conduct the interview near the clubhouse.

But a couple of days before our session Mt. St. Helens blew her top, spewing volcanic ash and dust as far away as North Dakota. Mr. Welk suffers from a mild respiratory problem, and so his doctor suggested he avoid dust-filled air as much as possible — including outdoor interviews on golf courses.

We learned of the change late in the evening the day before we were scheduled to shoot. Prairie Public TV had no studio in Bismarck in 1980, so we began a frantic search for a location.

We thought of the large, comfortable living room at the governor's residence, where we'd interviewed Governor Art Link and his wife Grace a few months earlier. Why not? We called Walt Dockter, his staff assistant, who promptly replied, "No problem. What time will you get here?"

Welk arrived precisely at nine o'clock, accompanied by his longtime friend and golfing partner Rolly Hogue II of Linton. Rolly had been instrumental in arranging the interview. In a letter, Welk wrote him in part, "The public TV interview idea sounds fine — but then, things are always fine when I put myself in your hands. You have always used good taste and good judgment, and I know you always will." I quietly hoped I wasn't putting Rolly on the spot.

I had read Welk's books and nearly everything written about the man in the past fifteen years, and I felt I knew this person I was going to interview. But to know Lawrence Welk, you truly must meet him face to face.

The simple charm and warmth that seems to transcend the television screen are really something to behold in person. He smiles and laughs easily. The thick German-Russian accent evokes memories of conversations overheard long ago when hired hands gathered to scrub up at the water trough after a day in the fields. There is a quiet pride, completely without arrogance, that comes from a job well done. Lawrence Welk is genuinely flattered when you ask him to tell his story.

As we waited for the cameras to begin to roll, I asked him if I could call him Lawrence during our conversation. He insisted on it. I quipped, "Fine — and you can call me 'Mr. Christenson'." My feeble attempt at humor was lost, however. He did just that for the first few moments of our conversation until I sheepishly told him, "'Boyd' will be fine."

*In an article in **Women's Home Magazine** back in 1973, your daughter Donna was quoted as saying, "The Welks aren't so talented. They are just persistent."*

Is that a pretty good summary of how you've succeeded in your remarkable career?

Yes, I remember when she said that. I think she was quite right. Persistence — that is so true.

I am so very fortunate because a great many people do something in life that they really don't enjoy doing. Some of them are even bugged by what they do. I am the opposite: I love what I am doing.

I love it so much that I promised my wife and my children I would retire at sixty-five. . .and I am a little past that right now!

You have had many high points and low points in your career. One that turned out to be a combination of low and high was in 1971, when ABC-TV cancelled the television show you had had for many years. You commented later that was one of the lowest points in your life.

It was.

You know, to start with, in the orchestra business, in the show business, people always tell you how good you are doing. The rating is good, and they keep saying, "We wouldn't think of missing your show." Then all of a sudden you get cancelled! That's a little different cup of tea.

But it's possible that that was the best thing that has ever happened to me.

You went on from there to the largest audiences of your career, even bigger audiences than you had before.

Oh, yes — much bigger than before. When we were with ABC we really thought we were doing good. But it was after that, when we got cancelled, that we created our own network, and that is the thing that gave us our long life on television.

Your career had another low point back in about 1931 in a place called Dallas, South Dakota. The band you had at that time all picked up and left you. Tell us about that.

I had a small band in those days. I had a five-piece band with Homer Schmidt, a very good drummer; Leo Fortin, a trumpet player who is from Waubay, South Dakota; Cliff Moe, who played saxophone, and Rollie Chestney, a very good piano player who was very popular with the ladies.

All of a sudden they called me in and told me that they decided to go on without me. They felt like I was holding them back, because my speech was questionable and my accordion-playing was questionable. I think Leo Fortin was the leader of them all. He still lives in South Dakota and has tried to make a comeback several times since then. They went on by themselves but they never really made it.

It was really a tremendous decision but I decided to go on, too. Years ago, the "Billboard" magazine used to have a list of the musicians that were available or wanted. I saw the "Billboard" and I noticed some musicians available in Ohio, two of them, a saxophone player and a trumpet player. I sent them a wire and they said they could come right away.

So right away I had a little three-piece band again, and I started over. But through that time, those three or four days, I was afraid I would have to go home back on the farm. My father had told me he could see me coming back this way, in rags, and I just didn't want that to happen, so I started again.

And it was amazing. The second time around, things went much better.

In referring to your organization today, you always talk about your "musical family." You have a set of rules or a family plan, as you would call it, that has worked very well for you, hasn't it?

Tremendously, yes. What it really is, is a family type of organization. I am the father and I look at my musicians and singers as my children.

I give them one year's trial. If they make that one year, I start sharing the business with them. I don't share alike with all of them. I share in proportion to how valuable they make themselves. So we have competition there constantly, and it's a healthy competition.

Everyone tries to work themselves up as far as they can. And some of the worst people that I have had years back are some of the best people that I have today. It does work from the standpoint of developing talent.

In one of the four books you have written — I believe it was in **Ah-One and Ah-Two** *— you talked about another low point in your career, also in 1971, when your band was not playing up to its potential. You became a little disgusted, a little disappointed in their performance, and in fact threatened to throw in the towel if things didn't change. It was a very crucial time for you.*

You sure have a good memory!

Yes, that was a real tense moment. I think an organization every once in awhile starts coasting, and of course you can't coast if you want to build a good show or band. There's a lot of work involved, a lot of dedication, and a lot of learning you have to do constantly.

It looked like I was in the doghouse with all of my people for a little while but I was strong in my talking with them. I told them, "If we are going to stay in the business, we are going to have to give the folks the best that's in our hearts." I wanted that.

You went home that night and had a very important phone call. Somebody called and said, "Gee, I am having trouble sleeping," and you said, "Gee, so am I." It was one of the guys from the group, and he said, "You know, Lawrence, you're right."

You have a better memory than I do!

So you said you turned over and you finally went to sleep.

I suppose in situations like that you're demonstrating your reputation as a stern taskmaster. You say the reporters usually ask about it rather hesitantly. Is that a fair description?

In a sense, yes, it could be. In another sense it is possible that I have less strict rules than anyone that has ever operated.

But if the show starts at nine o'clock or whatever time it is, they all have to be there. If they aren't there, and if I would allow them, they would fall apart right then and there. So I am quite strong and I do have certain rules that you have to live up to.

What do you look for when you audition, say, a couple of dancers, a singer or a saxophone player? What qualities do you watch for in those people?

Something that the public would enjoy — that's the basis of it. Not something that I would just enjoy myself.

I am always looking at the public. They are my audience. They are the people who believe in me, and I have to please them when they come to see us, or when they tune us in. That's not easy to do.

I make decisions basically to play the music they like. I know this. I am basically a Dixieland jazz man, but if I would play only Dixieland jazz on the show, there wouldn't be a show. I sometimes cheat a little bit — out of twenty numbers I play one Dixieland number. But most of what I play will please the audience, I hope.

Your wife Fern says she thinks that your secret is that you genuinely like people and you genuinely trust people until they give you some reason not to trust them.

I think that's a good analysis. I like all people. I trust all people. Then when they prove themselves to be on the other side, though, I might not hang onto them.

Your wife also says that you groan every time you hear yourself talking on television. Is she referring to the German accent which has been with you since your childhood?

Yes. I had a difficult time to start with. In fact, I didn't want to talk at all. When I first started out they asked me to talk, I said, "No, no, no, that's out completely." I just didn't think I would be able to talk. But it was forced onto me. It was one of the most difficult things in my lifetime.

When I did start talking, which was at the Riverside Theatre in Milwaukee, a place I played, the people always laughed in the wrong places. I always used to ask, "What are you laughing at?"

In your autobiography, the best-seller **Wunnerful, Wunnerful**, *you painted a beautiful picture of what it was like growing up on a small North Dakota farm back at the turn of the century. And you also tell that you found out very early on that you didn't like the idea of being a farmer.*

I really didn't. Somehow I just couldn't quite stomach it, or face this idea of working in the manure in the barn. Things like that just didn't make a hit with me. And I wanted music more than anything else.

Where did the music thing start? I know your father played an accordion. You kids used to gather around his feet in the evening, and he would play to you. Is that when you were first exposed to music?

I would say that the music was possibly born into our family tree, maybe a long time back. Both my mother and my father had music in them. But in the olden times when they didn't have a country, when they had to go here and there, it was difficult for them to really bring it out.

My mother was a very good singer, although she would never sing in public. She was also an exceptionally good dancer. My mother was as good a dancer as any of the girls that I dance with on the show. But she never wanted to do it in public, nowhere except at home in our living room.

You mentioned that the accordion that your grandfather had once belonged to a shirttail ancestor of yours back in Odessa or Alsace-Lorraine who was a street player, a strolling minstrel.

That's right.

He had double-jointed thumbs and fingers, and you've said you had the same kind of hands.

I wish I had the same kind of hands — I have bones in mine!
They would talk about him, how he could take his fingers and put them back here, and all of those types of things. He was a blind man and music is all he ever did. He was exceptionally good at accordion. So I never got that good, and that's why I hire so many fine musicians.

This brings up another point. Once in a conversation I had with Myron Floren, whom you hired for your band many, many years ago, he told me it took a very special musician to hire an accordion player who was better than he was. How many musicians are secure enough to do that, I wonder?

I think it's important that a person know. . . "know thyself," I guess would be the right thing. I haven't had a chance to practice now for the last twenty or thirty years, and I know that if your are going to play on a coast-to-coast show you really have to be prepared. I wasn't in a position to prepare because there are so many other things that you have to do on the management side.

That's the reason I hired Myron Floren. I was very sold on him. I was playing down in St. Louis in the local ballroom there, and Myron came out one night. I had known him from back in South Dakota; he was a farm boy too. I got him up on the stage and had him play, and that's the worst mistake I ever made! After he finished playing I found myself underneath the piano!

Let's go back to the farm for a moment, Lawrence.
This was early on — you were probably sixteen or seventeen years old. You'd just purchased a couple of fifteen-dollar accordions that lasted you about a week or a week and a half, and you decided that you had to have a better instrument for four hundred dollars. You made a very important deal with your father at that time. . .

It was a tough deal, but maybe one of the best.

I wanted a good accordion because the reeds kept breaking on those cheap accordions all the time. I told my father that if he would buy me the real good accordion, the best accordion that was available, I would stay on the farm until I was twenty-one years of age.

I waited four years for that day to come up. But it was a good thing that I stayed there because while I stayed on the farm I kept playing all the time. When my brothers and sisters said, "Lawrence, we can't stand it anymore," I would go out and play for the animals.

You mentioned that you could almost fill the hall with rabbits and maybe a couple of sheep who came to hear you play.
You had a very serious illness also early on in your life. Didn't it kind of dictate the direction you were going to take?

Ruptured appendix, right here at the hospital in Bismarck.

You convalesced a long, long while. Tell us about that.

I was at St. Alexius Hospital for seven weeks, and for three more months after that I was at home with a tube in my side draining out the poison. I wasn't able to go to school that year at all.

By the next year I was so much taller than the rest of the people that would have gone into the fifth grade. It wasn't too difficult to talk your parents into not going to school if you were willing to work at home, and that's exactly what I did. I stayed on the farm and worked and kept my music going, which I wanted more than anything else.

Was there some point along the line or some particular moment in your musical career when you said, "This is the turning point; I think I can make it as a professional musician; I think I can make a living at this"?

I don't think so. I don't think so. I don't think that I was like all the people that want to shoot up into the big time at one shot.

I only wanted to play. That's all I wanted to do, was play. I was ready to play at all times.

You worked with one gentleman who was a little late with the paychecks. In fact, you left him once and then you came back.

Yes — Lincoln Boulds and his Chicago Band. I can mention that because he is not with us anymore.

You must have asked yourself why you stayed with him so long. What kept you coming back? What was it about him that you admired so much?

Well, it was because he gave me an opportunity to play and I appreciated that very much. He had one extremely bad habit, and that was that on payday you could never find him.

Another gentleman in those same years became quite a hero of yours, George. . .

George Kelly. I am here today on the account of two years I had a chance to spend with George T. Kelly, playing all of the little towns here in North Dakota.

I admired his showmanship. He was the kind of a man that was a natural comedian. He could go out and talk to the people while I made my changes and just keep them in stitches.

I think that without the two years I spent with him I might have never made it. He was a tremendous showman.

You have been on the music scene for a number of decades and you have seen all kinds of music come and go, fads and different styles. Was there ever a time in your career when you thought that maybe you'd have to change the style of your music a little bit to keep pace with the times?

No. I am basically a Dixieland jazz man, as I've said, but I'm a disciplined man as well, and I am a believer in playing for my audience so they will understand what I do.

I have never really played as much Dixieland jazz as I'd like, except for maybe one number in a show. But it's my own favorite music for sure. Sometimes when I play the records at home, I may start about at nine o'clock and still be playing Dixieland at two in the morining, because I love it so much. But it's something that I never overdo in my shows.

One of the classic publicity photos of you was taken when you put on the hippie vest and the big strings of beads and the hippie wig. What was the occasion for that?

Well, in the show business you try to come up with humorous types of things. I did that when the hippies first came in. I made myself up like a hippie when we played in one town. The man who hired me was standing on the outside of the dressing rooom. When I had all my stuff on, I went out there and talked to him. He was mad at me about something; he was really telling me what a terrible man I am. He didn't even recognize me.

I went up on the stage for a little bit with this same outfit on, and that's the coldest audience I ever found.

Your fans didn't like that.

Not at all, not until I took that wig off.

You are seventy-six years of age. Yet I am looking at your schedule here for the month of June. Your concert schedule starts in Oakland, California, on the sixth and then it runs the sixth, seventh, eighth and ninth. . .well, eighteen straight days from Oakland, California, to Lincoln, Nebraska.

People would ask, "How do you get the energy, the physical and mental energy to do a concert schedule of that kind?" More importantly, how do you keep up your enthusiasm?

Of course, but you have me wrong, Boyd. You think I am seventy-six. I am actually seventy-seven.

Then it's even more so. How do you do it?

I think when you like what you are doing, that helps a great deal. I think that's one thing that perhaps we should study up on nowadays. Rather than making people just take a job for the money, I think if we could get them into the kind of job that they like, they'd have a better chance to make good at it.

Let's go back again to 1971, when ABC cancelled your contract and you were forming the Lawrence Welk Network and going into syndication. One other question that newsmen asked you quite frequently was, "Why don't you quit when you are ahead?" You certainly didn't need the money. You were at an age when a lot of people think about retiring. It's the same kind of question they'd maybe like to ask Bob Hope or George Burns.

In my particular case it might be a little bit different than for either of them.

I look at my musical family pretty much as that — my family. They have been with me for such a long time, and they look toward me a little bit like I am responsible for them. If I would retire, I am not so sure whether they could do so well.

I have one hundred people working for me, about fifty people around the studio and all this, and another forty-five or fifty in the orchestra. So if it would appear to me to be enough that I have done well in the show business — that I am okay as far as myself, and the heck with you fellows — that wouldn't be my cup of tea. I don't feel that way about it.

So you feel the responsibility to your family.

Not really 'feel a responsibility' as such. But I figure that as long as I'm feeling good and as long as Mrs. Welk will okay it, I will stay with my musical family.

And I must say that when my band operates at the high level of efficiency and perfection, there's nothing that brings me more joy and happiness than being in front of them.

You mentioined that you can be tired and kind of down, mentally and physically, and yet as soon as you get on that stage, it's like new life is being pumped into you somehow.

Right. I think we have today perhaps some of the best musicians in the world, and it's a great joy to go on in front of them and lead them through their pieces.

Isn't it fair to say you're giving your group greater and greater responsibilities? You told me that you really should be in Escondido right now getting ready for taping a television show, but that you will instead come in the day of the taping because you have people who can pick up the loose ends.

I think people are involved better that way. You have to let them do it themselves.

Let them make some mistakes, and then come in and clean them up, but clean them up in such a way so you don't hurt them. Do it through kindness, rather than with a strong arm.

Back in the old days after Glenn Miller passed from the scene, there was still the Glenn Miller Band directed by Tex Beneke. As some of the big bands' leaders dropped by the wayside, someone else would come and want to take their place. Do you ever envision the day when there will be a Lawrence Welk Orchestra without Lawrence Welk?

To me it would be a great thing if I could turn my band over to one of the members who would keep it going. I have tried it already, in fact, and discussed it with different people.

But most of the people who have hired me don't seem to want the band unless I am there.

This has been one of my problems. If I don't go along with the band myself, there's a different situation out there.

You have another love in addition to music. . .you still spend a lot of time out on the golf course, don't you?

I am glad you brought that up! I pretty near shot a thirty-nine the other day here in Bismarck. Yes — and then on that last hole, I went in the water.

Don't you play a few celebrity tournaments?

Yes, I play quite a few of them.

When did you take up the game of golf?

I took up the game of golf years ago because my health was very bad. I went out and started playing to get exercise and fresh air. In the show business it's good just to get away from the big crowds, and get out there and live like regular people do.

I have an idea that I am still here today on account of golf. I think if I wouldn't have taken up the game, I would have been gone a long time ago.

*One final question. In an interview you gave to **U.S. News and World Report** in 1977, of all magazines, you said the free enterprise system is in danger and that it would be difficult for anyone to follow the path you took. Tell us more about that.*

Young people don't have the freedom anymore that we had when I started out.

There were no unions where I started. I was able to play in Hague, North Dakota, and sell tickets myself — you know, for anything I could get. And then I went on to Aberdeen. I went to Watertown, South Dakota. I went to Yankton, Sioux City, Omaha. You weren't bothered by unions there.

Today if someone my age in those days would want to start, you couldn't do what you wanted to. You would have to do what the union tells you to do. You would have to go and get so much money from everybody.

Years ago when I started, I just took out ten or fifteen percent for my expense for car and gasoline. I split what was left with the rest of the band. You couldn't do that today.

The unions are so strong today, and it's a different cup of tea. We have lost to some degree — or maybe a large degree — the free enterprise system.

You have a wonderful musical family, and you have been a wonderful musical father to them. We wish you continued success.

Thank you very, very much — and I thank you very much Boyd, for visiting with me today. It just shows how beautiful and friendly our state is.

We love the people that we get from here. I have hopes that in the future, if we continue our show, we will be so lucky that we can always include a few people from North Dakota. This is still where they have the best people.

To use a very famous phrase. . ."wunnerful, wunnerful."

That's beautiful but you forgot something.

(He makes the sound of a champagne cork popping out of the bottle.)

Can you do that?

(Boyd imitates the sound.)

Hey, I like your sound better!

Maybe you can hire me and take me on the road.

You are hired.

Milton Young

In 1983 North Dakota lost a man who was one of the most significant political figures of the state's history — U.S. Senator Milton Young, who retired from politics in 1980 after serving thirty-five years and ten months in the United States Senate.

Until I was old enough to know better, I thought that North Dakota telephone poles were erected with a "Reelect Milt Young" poster already in place.

Some years ago I had the pleasure of introducing the senator at the dedication of the northern North Dakota water project which bears his name, and I told him the telephone story. He nodded and said, "Maybe we should have thought of that."

On another occasion I introduced him at a dinner by saying, "I don't know how long Milt Young has been in the Senate, but the man he replaced was named Moses." The line, which drew a great laugh, was of course true. The reference was to John Moses, the former North Dakota governor whose unexpired term Young was named to fill in 1944.

When Young's age became an issue in the 1974 Senate race, one of his campaign directors lightheartedly offered to buy the "Moses line" to take it out of circulation; out of respect for the man North Dakotans called "Mr. Wheat" I retired it voluntarily.

Art Linkletter once told me during an interview that the best conversations are with kids under ten years of age and women over the age of sixty-five. He explained, "Kids under ten will tell you anything because they don't know better, and women over sixty-five don't give a damn."

To that list I would add politicians on the brink of retirement.

My conversation with the senator was taped a few weeks before the presidential election of 1980. He volunteered the information that the Select Subcommittee on Appropriations, *of which Young was a member, "has to hide all the money for intelligence purposes and new weapons." Young talked about "two new weapons which are startling." The senator did not go into detail, but did say that one of them had "become so big that pretty soon it will have to be made public."*

Shortly before that November's election a story broke nationwide that the United States was working on a remarkable airplane capable of flying undetected by radar called the Stealth bomber. My assumption is that the airplane was one of the "startling weapons" Milt Young told North Dakota about in our conversation that fall.

If I were to list the records that you have set and your accomplishments, we could spend the whole half hour doing that. But I think that we can tell the people that when you complete your term on the third day of January, 1981, you will have served for thirty-five years and ten months, longer than any Republican senator in history. I believe that only six senators in the history of the United States have served longer. So you have become an institution now. . .like the Washington and the Lincoln Monuments, you might say!

Boyd, I have served the longest uninterrupted term as a Republican. One Republican did serve a year and a half longer, but he took a break in there. That was a senator from Wyoming.

You had to make a rather critical decision in 1974 about whether to seek reelection. You thought about that, I know, a long, hard time. I think you may have wanted to step down in 1974. If you had it to do over, would you have made the same decision, Senator, to run again?

I think that under the circumstances, I would. My opposition and some within the Republican Party itself felt that I should not run for reelection because a poll had been taken that they thought showed that I couldn't win.

My Democratic opponents used the wrong strategy, though. They said that I couldn't be reelected. That become a sort of challenge. It bothered me, because I had only wanted to serve in such a way that when it came time to quit, I could still feel that I could be reelected.

It's sort of a stigma to leave office because you couldn't win again. That really was what prompted me to run again. At least, it started that way.

That's like ringing the old fire bell and the horses are ready to answer the call! So they used the wrong strategy, obviously, in 1974.

It was their own strategy, but it backfired. They made it difficult for me to quit.

You have been very involved throughout the years in the Garrison Diversion project to bring water from the Missouri River to farms and cities east of the reservoir. You have said that you feel it's one of the most important things that you have worked on in all the years you've served in Washington. Now, as you are just weeks away from leaving the Senate, what do you feel is the prognosis for Garrison Diversion right now?

Well, it's all right for the time being, but there are two major problems that we have to resolve in the future. One is that of acquiring mitigation land. The requirements have been changed. They want only drained land, and the farmers just can't part with that kind of land.

Another one is with Canada. I think that we are going to be able to solve many of our differences. The first hurdle now is construction of the Lonetree Reservoir. The Canadians are opposing it, but the International Joint Commission went on record and said that Lonetree Reservoir could be constructed without hurting Canada's water resources. The construction can be handled in the way as proposed by the IJC.

Do you foresee Garrison ever becoming the project someday that you and others have envisioned for so many years?

Yes, I think it will. It's becoming more and more important, though, for cities than for irrigation itself. There are many cities now that are looking towards Garrison Reservoir as a future water supply.

You are optimistic, then.

Yes, and I think the need for water will be even greater in the western part of the state, where you have the huge deposits of coal. You have to bring water together with coal to develop the energy that our country needs.

Some months ago you had a much-ballyhooed difference of opinion with Congressman Mark Andrews that made the headlines in the North Dakota newspapers for a number of weeks. What was that about? Can we talk about that for a minute?

We have had some differences from time to time. I think that one started over Garrison Diversion. The Jamestown **Sun** carried a headline that said "Andrews Favors Zero Funding."

Maybe he didn't say that, but that's what the story said. And then when President Carter made the announcement of his budget containing no funds for the project, the Congressman said he thought that we could live with that. I do think he probably meant "without all" of it, but we misunderstood each other. We got into quite an argument over that.

Congressman Andrews has been criticized in some circles for giving up a great deal of seniority in the House of Representatives to run for the seat you occupy in the Senate. How do you feel about that criticism?

It's really up to him and the people of North Dakota. I can't blame him for wanting to go to the Senate. But he has been the only member representing the state in the House, where seniority isn't as powerful as being an able legislator. And we are giving up something. But maybe we will be making up in the Senate what we lost in the House.

The seniority system has been cussed and discussed for years and years and years. How do you answer criticism of the seniority system? What are the pros and cons of that system of leadership in Congress?

There's really no substitute for it. It's used in labor organizations, church organizations, business organizations — everyone uses it. You have to.

For example, when Congressman Andrews goes to the Senate, he will have served seventeen years in the House and he will have seniority over all the other new members elected to the Senate this year. That will give him a better break and better committee assignments to start with. That's one of the many examples.

You mentioned committees. That's a very important part of the role of a senator, being assigned to various committees. You are the ranking member of the Appropriations Committee, for example. What does it mean, with your seniority and your years in the Senate, to be on the Appropriations Committee? What does it mean you are able to do for, say, not only North Dakotans but people everywhere.

How much power does a chairman wield, I guess I am asking.

The chairman can wheel and deal with more power than the ranking member. But the chairman and the ranking member of the Senate Appropriations Committee and the subcommittees work very closely together.

When you mark up a bill — that's writing up a bill — you confer as to the things that you are going to put into it. The chairman and the ranking member sit down together with the staff and make recommendations for the subcommittee, then, and what position they take makes a awful lot of difference.

It's really a much more powerful position than most people realize.

Most of the decisions have been made and hammered out to a great degree, then, before the bill even gets to the floor for debate?

On some bills I work with, the subcommittee often makes no changes at all, the committee makes few changes, and little or no change is made on the Senate floor itself. On others, of course, the opposite is true.

I think that most members in the Senate are reluctant to oppose the position taken by the chariman and ranking member unless they have a good reason for it. They try to give you a little more consideration.

A North Dakota reporter once told me that North Dakotans have a history of reelecting their representatives for as long as they want to go back to Washington. The record does point that out. Other than the fact that you are doing a great job, how do you analyze this tendency to keep sending that same person back to the House or back to the Senate term after term, whenever they run for reelection?

It's a little difficult to analyze it.

In a state with a smaller population, a member of Congress — either of the House or the Senate — has closer contact with his people. He can help them more, and that's an advantage.

There are many advantages to serving in the Senate. Take the use of the boxholder privilege for mailing everything to voters at no charge. Senator Langer told me one time that with the boxholder mailing privileges, if you were defeated it was your own fault.

You mentioned Bill Langer — we can't get out of this discusssion without you telling me a Langer story or two, since you were a contemporary of his. You knew Bill very well.

One of the most outstanding I remember was when former Governor Aandahl was a congressman and his supporters wanted him to run for the Senate against Langer. He didn't want to and the family didn't want to, but finally out of party loyalty he became a candidate.

Since Aandahl had appointed me to the Senate, I thought that I should go out and try to get him elected. Senator Langer and I tangled in that campaign more than Senator Langer and Aandahl.

We wouldn't speak much during a campaign, but afterwards we would be all right again. But after that one, Bill wouldn't speak to me at all. One day they had a rural telephone meeting at the Powers Hotel in Fargo, and Senator Langer and I were both there. They called on me first. I said, "Langer is the most ungrateful person in North Dakota. I campaigned against him in all the counties except three, and those three that I didn't campaign in were the only ones that he lost."

Then we were on good terms again. I even endorsed him the last time he ran.

You had an interesting conversation with Senator Langer and, I believe, Congressman Usher Burdick in the cloakroom of the Senate one time. The outcome of what was discussed could have changed the course of North Dakota political history. Why don't you tell us about that?

Boyd, I think this is the first time I have ever told this story. It is interesting in a way.

Senator Langer wanted me to meet with Congressman Usher Burdick in the Republican cloakroom. We had a little discussion there. That's when the Republicans were in control and Langer was the chairman of the Judiciary Committee, which had a lot to do with appointments.

Langer wanted to know if I would be interested in supporting Quentin Burdick, Usher's son, to be appointed judge. Was I interested in it? Usher was there and of course wanted to hear what I was going to say.

I said, "No, Quentin is a little too liberal for me, but I will support Gene Burdick, his brother."

I have often thought that if I had said "sure," Quentin might have been a judge today rather than a U.S. Senator.

What year was that?

It was in the early 1950s.

Before he was elected to the House for the first time. That's an interesting story.

Not so long before. . .four years or so.

You have gone through a number of eras in campaigning, from meeting in little town halls with the Farmers Union to using radio and television and very sophisticated means of campaigning. What was it like in those early years? You've told me that you once were a candidate for some position and you ended up campaigning in a couple of the wrong counties.

That's when I was in the State Senate. I got across the line into Stutsman County by mistake.

But one of the most interesting experiences was when, before my election of twelve years ago, they wanted me to speak up at Bottineau one evening. I told them we were going to be in Watford City that afternoon at an REA meeting and I couldn't make it. It was too far to drive.

They said that they'd send an airplane down for me. I asked, "Do you have lights up there to land by after dark?"

They answered, "No, but we will have cars with lights on."

So I hurried up and got in the plane, and I dozed off. When I woke up, it was dark and we were circling. Fortunately, the pilot had turned on the landing lights and we could read the sign on a country elevator. It said "Deloraine." I knew there's no town in North Dakota called Deloraine. It was Deloraine, Manitoba.

I said, "Where's Bottineau?"

He said, "Due south." So we started flying the other way against a stiff southeast wind, and pretty soon he was circling again. I asked where we were and he said, "Not sure."

I asked, "How's the gas?"

He said, "Well, if we have to we can land at Minot."

So he finally said, "I think I will stop at a farmhouse and find out where we are at," and he landed in a cornfield only about a quarter of a mile from a house.

He was from the Bronx in New York, and an excellent pilot, but he wasn't acquainted with the country. But he wanted to get back in the plane and go on to Bottineau for the picture-taking.

I remember your last line: "I think we will drive the last leg of the journey."

You have been privileged to work with a number of presidents, dating back to Truman and Eisenhower, and through

Nixon and Ford. I am sure you met and talked with President Roosevelt, didn't you?

No, he was at Warm Springs, Georgia, and very ill when I was appointed. I was appointed March 12, 1945, and he died, I think, April 14.

Who are the presidents that stand out most in your mind?

I think one of the best presidents of my time was General Eisenhower. The most colorful one, though, was President Johnson.

President Johnson would ask you to do a lot of personal things. The first time Lyndon was a candidate for president, he called me over to the White House and he said, "I want you to get some delegates for me from North Dakota."

I said, "How in the hell can I get some? I am Republican." It didn't make a bit of difference to him. And you know, I think I did help him get one, at that.

I was over at the White House quite often when he was president. One day he said, "I want you to go back and make a farm speech." I told him that the bill he wanted me to talk about had passed about three weeks before. He said, "It doesn't make a damn bit of difference." He wanted me to make that farm speech anyway. I went back and wrote about a twenty-minute speech, just like he said.

You must have so many memories we can't touch upon even a small number in this half hour. This question has to be asked: when you step down in 1981, is there a possibility that we will see a book about your life in the Senate?

A lot of people have suggested that, Boyd, and a history teacher at the University of North Dakota had been doing some interviews and may be writing a biography someday.

I never have kept a diary or been much for notes. But there are so many interesting things that I could mention that I think we could have an interesting story, with eight presidents and spread over nearly thrity-six years.

I am sure there are stories that you could tell that can only be told when you are no longer a United States Senator — is that fair to say?

Many of them, Boyd.

For about the last twelve years I have been on the Select Subcommittee on Intelligence Appropriations, in which we have to hide all the money for intelligence purposes and new weapons. We bury this money in unrelated appropriations bills. Only about two or three of us in the Senate know the amount of money and even for the purpose.

Right now we are in the process of developing two new weapons which are startling, I think, exceptionally good ones.

The unfortunate thing, I think, is that we have developed weapons in the past, like the B-1 bomber, that could be good. But when we come to produce them, they seem to run out of money.

But you say we are working on a couple of super weapons right now that are not public knowledge at this point?

Not public knowledge. We have been hiding money for one of them that has become so big that pretty soon it will have to become public.

When you say "hiding the money," how is that done?

Well, for example, in the budget item for operations and maintenance. That's the biggest part of the defense appropriations bill. We will put maybe a billion dollars' worth of intelligence money in there, or in new projects.

A lot of times when it gets on the floor of the Senate, someone will want to cut operations and maintenance, thinking it's too big, or some other part of the bill where we've hidden money. The only thing we can do, the two of us, is to take them aside and tell them, "We've got some intelligence money in there."

Is that the kind of practice that a member of Congress could be criticized for? I am sure you have been in the past.

Criticized in some quarters, because they want everything public. But new weapons — you just can't make them public. We can't take everything we are doing and tell the public.

So there is a line that has to be drawn somewhere on the people's right to know.

I think more and more people have come to realize that.

The CIA has a real problem in this right-to-know thing. They get hundreds of requests, many of them from foreign countries' spies and whatnot, and they have had to answer them. But the law has been recently changed so that it cuts down their requests by about two-thirds.

We have seen in the last decade Watergate and the subsequent investigation, and the results of that. Now we have headlines of Billy Carter and his Libyan connection. We have had the FBI and their scam operations and the bribing of senators and congressmen.

Is our government under closer scrutiny from all quarters in this last decade than in previous times?

Boyd, I think that Congress is under closer scrutiny by both its own intelligence and especially by the press. The investigative press has been responsible for digging up a lot of corruption and wrong-doing. We have more committees now in both houses of Congress that can investigate, and do investigate.

So I think yes, the scrutiny has increased a lot, but not necessarily the amount of problems. You hear a lot of bad stories about the Congress and the federal government now, but mostly because more of them are brought to light.

*In a tribute to you printed in the **Congressional Record**, Senator Burdick had some very nice things to say about you, and so did Senator Baker from Tennessee. He said, referring to you, "He has always recognized the value of political competition, but he has always placed the enduring public interest above any temporary partisan interest."*

That is a statement that encompasses quite a bit. I thought about that line, for example, when I asked you about your difference of opinion with Congressman Andrews. So maybe we could talk for just a moment or two on your relationship with your fellow senators and congressmen in Washington. How did you get along there with the other members of the North Dakota delegation?

Well, I think quite good. You have your differences of opinion. If you didn't have, you wouldn't be much of a delegation there. If you believe in something you have to fight for it, and when you fight for it you naturally create some or cause some ill feelings. But on the whole it's worked good.

Members of Congress usually have a pretty good sense of humor and not many of them remember too long because maybe the next day you'll be working together.

On the whole, the people elect good men to Congress. We have a lot of very intelligent young people now. But they operate very differently, more on their own, than they used to. We don't have those great orators like we use to have them, Senators Vandenburg and George and Barkley. The last great one was Dirksen.

We don't have that type of orator anymore. But they are intelligent, very effective people.

You talk about great orators. . .in your early political years, you had a speech impediment or a halting method of speech that was very pronounced, as I understand. That had to be a devastating thing for a shy North Dakota farm boy — to get up to speak in front of a crowd and have some trouble making yourself understood in those early years. How did you overcome that, Senator?

That was a terrible problem, and I haven't overcome it all by any means yet. But it's much better than it was.

Oftentimes when I am speaking in public, I have to be thinking about my speech about as much as what I am going to talk about. It was a real problem. I was a farmer, going from the farm into the fastest company in the political business. It wasn't easy.

Did it ever discourage you in your early political years so much that you thought that because of it, you would not be a politician?

Yes, there was a lot of discouragement. Once in awhile someone would say, "Milt, make a speech."

I would say, "I am no speaker."

But they always told me, "You make good speeches — short ones."

I remember Fred Aandahl telling me, "Milt, you are no orator, but you always give them something to think about." I would always try to remember that. When I would make a speech, I tried to give them something to think about afterwards. If it was just my ability as an orator, it would depress them.

Was there substance to the rumor that Milt Young might be a candidate for vice president some years ago? Didn't I read that somewhere?

No, I don't think so.

It seems to me that I read that somewhere in a column throwing out possible vice presidential candidates' names

Well, it could have once or twice. But my name came up quite often years ago as a possible Secretary of Agriculture.

All right. Would you have ever wanted to leave the Senate for that particular job?

No. I guess the job I have is as big as I can handle.

The farm population makes up about four percent of the electorate. That's not a very loud voice the farmer has, when it comes to going to the polls — just four percent. Doesn't that put the farmer at a disadvantage? Don't politicians sometimes, in an election year, pay lip service to the farmers because they know that with such a small share of the American vote the farmer is not going to make that much difference?

But it does make a big difference. There's only a small percentage — I think only two — in the Senate now who are actually farmers themselves. But there is a surprising amount of people in big places in government and industry who came from farms or have close relatives on farms, and most of them realize that production of food and fibre is the most important thing in the world.

All together, that gives us a stronger voice than many people think at first.

How about retirement plans for Senator Young? I know you like to play a little golf. How will you spend your extra time now that you are retiring?

I will certainly play a lot of golf. One nice thing about it will be that I will be able to play golf summer and winter. Now I have other schedules, and many times it's a beautiful day for golf and I can't play.

I will leave the Senate with mixed feelings. I will be able to enjoy life much more and get acquainted with my twenty great-grandchildren. That was twenty of them last week, I should say. I don't know how many I have by now!

Will Arizona be your retirement home?

It will be for the winters. The summers. . .I will spend the summers in North Dakota.

Do you still have some old cronies in your home town of LaMoure whom you can sit down around the cracker barrel with and talk about the old days?

Yes, there are a few of them left there.

I want to thank you for taking time out of your schedule to come and chat with us. As I mentioned at the outset, we could just touch on a few of the highlights in a career that has spanned thirty-five years and ten months in the United States Senate

— longer than any Republican has ever served, and longer than all but six senators in history. You have served with great distinction. And you have honored us with your presence.

Well, thank you, Boyd. I tried hard to do a good job.

Perhaps that last statement stands as an epitaph to Senator Young — a man who throughout his long life representing North Dakota in the United States Senate "tried hard to do a good job." Many in North Dakota, where the flags flew at half mast for the month after his death, would agree today that he achieved that goal.

Harold Schafer

Harold Schafer's philosophy is simple: "I like to call on people and talk to them and sell them things."

In 1940 he was doing just that. His product was floor wax — purchased by the barrel, bottled in the basement of a Bismarck paint store, and sold door-to-door by Schafer himself.

And people apparently like to buy things from Harold Schafer. By 1948 his Gold Seal Wax Company of Bismarck had expanded its business nationwide, and today the company has packaging and distribution centers on both coasts of the United States.

The company still sells some floor wax and has added to its line, among other items, bubbles for your bath water and bleach for your clothes.

Schafer doesn't rap on doors anymore. He gets his pitch to the consumer via a massive television ad campaign. And the people he talks to these days are often in the legal and accounting divisions of the company.

Schafer always takes the time to indulge his ready sense of humor. At a "roast" of Senator Mark Andrews and Quentin Burdick, he showed up wearing a long robe and a grotesque rubber mask. The audience was kept guessing about the identity of this mystery guest until Schafer was finally unmasked.

Senator Burdick later observed, "Harold, I haven't seen you looking so good in years."

Harold, you epitomize the traditional American dream — small boy who grew up poor but through his own hard work made it very, very big.

It's been a fun life for me, I can tell you that. It's been a real pleasure. Hard to describe the feelings that come when you look back after having lived it.

You told me the motto of your company is "Work." W-O-R-K. You were ingrained with that motto back in grade school days when you were working and making your own way.

For some reason or other, I like to work. I don't know — maybe it's nervous energy. Maybe it's frustration. Maybe it's some physical thing.

I was not particularly a great student and I am not particularly a great guy to tell other people what to do. But I have liked to work, and that's how I've lived my life, working, all along the line.

I became a salesman. It made sense; I like to call on people and talk to them and sell them things. So I guess that was really the beginning of the company. I have been doing it ever since I was a kid, and I am still doing it.

You enrolled at North Dakota State University back in the late 1920s when you were getting into what was known as the Great Depression. You worked at a number of jobs — in fact, you were making pretty good money when you were going to school.

Yes, actually I was making more money going to college here in Fargo than my fraternity brothers over there at the Alpha Gamma Rho house were making when they got out of school. On the other hand, my father had passed away in 1927 and I did have a younger sister in high school in Bismarck. I decided that it was more important that she got out of high school than that I get a college education. I left NDSU after a year or so to get full-time work to help out with money at home.

But making money, making enough money to live on was never any problem because of the way I worked.

Here in Fargo, I worked downtown at the Globe Clothing Store, and I would work there every day until they closed. In those days stores would usually close at six thirty; it was a quarter to seven before they got the door locked.

Then I would hike up to the north end of Broadway and work for Claude Miller in his filling station. After that, I would go to the Webster Cafe and wash glasses, and do the same thing once in awhile in the fraternity house. For a few weeks I even fed the white rats over at the chemistry building. Part of the time I'd get up a couple hours earlier than usual and deliver milk before dawn for the Weisser boys, who had milk routes.

In other words, I was just a general handyman, ready to do just whatever was available to do.

How did the Gold Seal Company start? We have heard stories that this was kind of a cottage industry, started in the basement of your home.

Actually, it started in the basement of Vantine Paint and Glass in Bismarck, North Dakota. I used to buy barrels of floor wax from Minnesota Mining in St. Paul and pour it into glass bottles that I bought at Finney's Drugstore in Bismarck. The guy who owned Bismarck Business College, Professor Jack, printed all my labels for nothing because his students had to have experience typing. I put them on those bottles and sold the wax myself door-to-door.

Finally I was selling more than I could package myself. I had six high school boys working in Vantine's basement after school and Saturday and Sunday, just bottling that wax.

As the business grew, by 1943 I found out that there were such things as contract packagers — that's people who will package things for you just the way you want them. So I bought some more merchandise or had it made for me, and then, as a salesman, I went out and sold it.

I read a story about your trying to sell to a local hardware store, and helping the owner to unload a truck. . .

I did that, actually, when I started. When you work as a salesman in these little stores, you find out right away that the merchant is busy. Having worked in a lot of stores myself, it was easy for me to help putty a window in the back room or to fill a shelf with merchandise, and so I did that. They often bought from me afterwards — but not always.

There's a book called **Sixty Great Sales Stories By Sixty Great Salesmen**. When they invited me to contribute to it, I wrote that little story you mention about my experience in Aberdeen, South Dakota.

When I went there I totally failed. Somehow or other, it was a cold community and I didn't have the right story. My man who was with me made calls at the same time, and he didn't make nay sales, either. We sort of hung our heads and cried on each other's shoulders.

After a couple days he had to leave because his daughter had to go to the hospital for an appendicitis operation. I was left in Aberdeen all alone. It was a kind of lonesome night! But I made up my mind I was not going to leave until I'd made a sale there.

The next morning I found a merchant who was unloading a carload of lumber at his lumber yard. Right out of the clear blue sky, I found myself helping this guy unload his lumber, and later on in the morning he bought a big bunch of goods from me.

I went around Aberdeen, I think, for the rest of that week and sold forty-three different customers. I never did call on another one that I didn't sell. It was a fascinating experience.

You mention that cold, lonely night. There had to be some moments in your business that made you search your soul a little. Were you ever discouraged enough to think of giving it up?

Oh, yes, a few times. There's no doubt about that in the early days. I think that maybe I came closest after the first couple of years — because that's when I ran out of money and that's when I started sponging on my friends. That's a sort of annoying thing in a normal man's mind!

But I began to do better after I had found a supplier that could make goods for me and all I had to do was to sell them. My success rate became a little better. I made enough money to live on. Then I reached the point where I earned enough to hire a couple men to work for me. I finally wound up covering the territory from Duluth, Minnesota, to Salt Lake City, Utah, with about fourteen men working for me.

We were selling merchandise and doing a good little job in that territory before we went national in 1948.

OK, that leads to my next question. Was there ever a time when you came running home and said to your wife, "We are going to make it"?

Oh, yes. Williston, North Dakota. I'd made $100 in one day.

Was that the moment?

That was the moment. And Billings, Montana, in 1945 when I sold the first full carload of goods I ever sold in my life.

Then you knew you were off and running?

Then you had the feeling of confidence that what you were doing was all right.

How about after those lean years at the beginning — after the thing took off and you started making some money, did you indulge yourself or your family in any special way?

Oh, I don't think there is any question about that! You are exposed to the beautiful windows in shopping places all over America, especially when you travel and call on customers there.

If you have little girls at home, it's awful easy to buy those little girls pretty things. It's awful easy to buy your wife something nice. That's, I think, a very normal thing.

I started driving a little nicer car. I started buying a little more expensive clothes for myself. I think those things are normal. You don't pay quite so much attention to every penny.

On the other hand, those pennies were come by the hard way, and you watch them pretty close for a long time because it's habit.

Tell us, where is Gold Seal today? Hasn't it gotten larger than a lot of people in North Dakota even realize it is?

We think we are on a fresh roll with a growing operation.

My company is making some changes. My son came into the business nine years ago, and took over the presidency of the company two years ago. Now, as I mentioned, I am a salesman. I am an extrovert. I like to talk; I like to sell. My son is a more careful man. He was a mechanic as a kid. He likes to take things apart and put them together again, and he knows what makes them tick inside. So he is bringing to our company a new dimension of carefulness, planning things carefully and executing them carefully, whereas I am a little more of what they call a shoot-from-the-hip type of cowboy.

In all of my early days we bought material and had it manufactured for us. My son has brought us to the point where we now have a factory of our own in Patterson, New Jersey, and another in Chicago. He and our lawyers and accountants have been on the West Coast recently, and we are hoping to have a manufacturing facility and a production operation in the area for our company before the year is over with.

America is a beautiful, big country. On the other hand, the products my company sells are somewhat heavy. Freight is a costly item. You can't make them in New Jersey and ship them across the nation like I could in 1942. You have to manufacture items fairly close to where they are consumed today. We have decided that we need three points of manufacture.

Of course, as the company grows we can now invest in a factory, and that's a different operation. You have your capital in the factory plant instead of in a carload of merchandise. But in the factory you deal with the raw materials, the packages, the tin cans and paper boxes and plastic containers — that's a whole different kind of operation. But it does give you more solid growth. You own your goods at a little better price. You have better quality control.

So we are actually looking forward to a great period for Gold Seal.

The 1980s have begun very well for our company. We are expanding a little bit. We are trying to introduce a few new products and buy a few other products that already are in the marketplace. We just feel that this is the time to push forth with the effort. We have expanded our executive staff by hiring some brains that we didn't happen to have within the company; that's just in the last couple of years.

We are planning a great future in the 1980s. We really are.

You mentioned your son Ed became president two years ago. That must give you a special feeling, for a father to turn the company over to the son.

I think it is special but not anything out of the ordinary. There are hundreds and hundreds of people whose sons have taken over the family business...downtown Fargo, downtown Bismarck, on farms all over North Dakota, in the little towns. In fact, I think we are fortunate in North Dakota because so many of our little businesses are in the third and fourth generation of father-to-son and father-to-son.

America has grown so big, and its corporations so big in the past thirty years, that this has gotten lost. Maybe the sons are still in a lot of them. But they got lost just because of the volume of people working there around them. They have thousands and thousands of employees; the son is in there someplace, but he may no longer be the one you can see.

Are you as active in the company today as you were, say, ten years ago?

I have been active for twenty-four hours a day, seven days a week for thirty-five years. I don't expect to ever change. It's just different activity these days.

I do a little more reading. I do a little more visiting, say, with the legal division of the company and the accounting division. I have many wonderful people who do a lot of good work for me.

We have had, of course, the normal turmoil. The Lord has taken some of the people that worked for us — some of them who were, unfortunately, even younger than I am. But at the same time we have a growing staff of young people around the age of my son, a little older and a little younger, that he is bringing into the company. They are giving us ambition and new excitement.

We are going to be able to use more help as we develop some plants and factories, and if we sell more products, we are going to need more salesmen. We are feeling pretty good about that.

My son is happy. I hope he is. . .he tells me so.

You told me earlier that you have a briefcase filled with work and that you came to Fargo a day early to get some time in your motel room to do some work. That was a pretty good-sized briefcase!

Well, we are no different than anybody else. We always have the perpetual problems with Uncle Sam and the Internal Revenue Service, and we have the perpetual problems of what are we going to do with what in the next year or two. That means matching personnel and matching people to jobs that need doing and figuring out who is capable and who isn't.

How about the business climate? We've heard so much about recession and inflation for the past few years. You certainly are very close to all of that from your vantage point. In simple terms, what's it like doing business in the U.S. today?

Business has been changing very fast in the last ten years. Everything is computerized; that ought to make it easier because you have more facts to make decisions on, and you have facts quicker than we used to have. In that way, it ought to be easier to run a business and expand business and do more business in the future than it has been in the past.

One frequent criticism is that government meddles too much in business. In your years with Gold Seal, have you agreed with that statement?

I think that is probably true. On the other hand, you and I can't sit here and condemn the government that we live under. If we don't like it, you know, it's a free world — we can go someplace else.

The government has been both good and bad to me in my day. We have been very successful in the courts of America, and we have had to be there a number of times to protect our right to be in business when challenged by some of our business competitors.

On the other hand, we have had difficulties with some of the divisions of government. We have had some plant construction stopped by OSHA which we thought was a little unreasonable. We have had some trouble with the Food and Drug Administration.

Really, though, I think that is part of the excitement of living and working in America. I don't think we can go home and sit down and say that we live in a lousy country because of something here or there. It is full of good people who want to work and they all are doing their thing. After all, we do have a good government. It has given us our ability to sit here and talk like this and enjoy life today. It is all possible and, believe me, there are countries where none of it is possible.

I get the feeling that Harold Schafer may have mellowed a bit over the years. Am I right?

You lose a little of the spark on that motor as the years go by.

Let's talk about politics a bit. Back in the early 1960s — was it 1962? — you were actively seeking the Republican nomination as a candidate for governor of North Dakota.

Yes, I actively sought to be governor of North Dakota.

I had a little political ambition. I suppose that comes because I was successful in business, though on the other hand I didn't particularly ever want it for selfish reasons. If I had any political power, I would probably try to use it to do some good for people. My life has been so good to me — the Lord's been so good.

As for my need or desire for a little fame and fortune, I have seen my name in the newspapers and I have seen my picture in the magazines. To want to be governor as an ideal or to have my picture taken standing in front of the Capitol — well, after all, I have already had my picture taken in front of the Capitol, and my picture hangs inside it. That doesn't make much difference to me at this point.

At that time I had a genuine desire to serve. I've followed up on that desire in other ways besides running for governor. I serve socially and I serve charities. I've been involved with Business Challenge, a summer program for high school youngsters. I work with North Dakota State Unviersity and I talk to an awful lot of high school classes. That all is public service, too, and I like to do it.

Was 1962 a personal disappointment for you?

I would say it perhaps was, at the moment, but certainly not at all anymore.

I have come to know many of the men in politics on both sides of the aisles; they have been personal friends of mine. They are all nice people, and certainly I didn't want to run for governor bad enough to fight with my friends to try to get it. I could have told you that ahead of time.

Some time ago in the "Bismarck Tribune" I saw a story that mentioned in the last paragraph that "Harold Schafer of Bismarck has also been mentioned as a possible gubernatorial candidate." In the last line it said, "Schafer was unavailable for comment today." I talked to you on the phone about two days later, and how did you react to that? Are you interested anymore?

I think it's wishful thinking. I certainly have no ideas about running. Several good Republican candidates are friends of mine and I am certainly not going to try to push them aside.

We have good Republican candidates for public office today, and I wish them much success. I am going to work for some of them.

We can't talk about Harold Schafer unless we mention Medora, North Dakota, which I know is one of your real pet projects. What has happened in that city? How did that all start?

That has been a thrill, really.

I bought the Rough Rider Hotel about twenty years ago and gave it to Russell Reid, the director of the State Historical Society.

He went to the Legislature to get some money to run this thing and maintain it, but they wouldn't give him any money. Russell was not a great salesman, you know, and he was not exactly an exciting person in public, though he was a great historian and certainly was a fantastic developer of the North Dakota Historical Society. He would be the creator of it, I guess you would have to say.

But somehow or another, he felt guilty about that old hotel. I was trying to give him the title to this piece of historic property but he couldn't do anything with it, because his hands were tied with the work he already had. He gave it right back to me.

So, like a crazy guy, I started running the Rough Rider Hotel myself. I tore it apart and put it together again. Then, of course, there wasn't any sewer or water in the city, so I had to put in some sewer and water. Then you can't have a hotel without having a dining room.

The first thing you know, I have a musical show in the hills. And then the people have to have bathrooms to go to and you have to have food to eat, and you have to have whiskey to drink and you have to have a place to sleep at night. So we wound up in the service industry in Medora, in the tourist business.

Medora is quite fascinating. It's attractive. It's different.

In selling Glass Wax and Snowy Bleach or Mr. Bubble, I can hold the product in my hand and I can hand it to you. In Medora I can talk about something that is out there in western North Dakota called the Badlands and all its fabulous history — but you and I can't see it. It's horse trading of a different kind. It's very fascinating.

My wife and I especially enjoy it. We entertain a tremendous number of people from foreign countries. At the show, we have registered the license plates of every state in America and every province in Canada now for three straight years. That's a real thrill. It's fun to talk to those people on the street about their visiting North Dakota.

I can tell by the way you are talking that Medora is a source of pride for you.

Yes, it is. It really is.

Any special plans for Medora in the coming years?

We are going to continue to expand Medora. It's part of the projected growth of the Gold Seal Company. It's just a matter of time, perhaps when construction costs in North Dakota level off from this impact of the energy business.

We will be adding some more motel units and some more campground units and some more entertainment features. We put in a new shooting gallery last year, and the city added a new swimming pool and tennis courts two years ago. We are going to do a little work in the theatre this year, improve the restroom facilities and the way you get up and down into your seats.

Medora is a living piece of North Dakota history, but it's also a town with a continual improvement program in its own right.

I have heard it referred to as "the town that Harold Schafer built." Is that fair to say?

Well, that's fair to say in one way. But on the other hand, everything Medora is blessed with first of all was made by the Lord. The Badlands have been there and will be there a long, long time.

I didn't mean to suggest that you made the beautiful Badlands!

Second, it's real. Teddy Roosevelt lived there and we didn't manufacture that. Harold Schafer didn't go off in the back room and say, "Well, we will build this beautiful hotel in here and we will build this store there." Those were created by real people. They lived in North Dakota.

Medora is a part of the heritage of the state. Our state is very proud that Teddy Roosevelt lived here, and we in Medora of course share that pride.

We feel that Medora is a living experience. I love the Badlands and always have. There's no place like them.

Shifting gears again, there's a cliche in our society that says, "Money can't buy happiness." How do you react to that? Can money buy happiness?

I don't think there's any question that it cannot.

You know, there are two kinds of millionaires, and I have had the experience of being both. There is a millionaire who has accumulated in his life a million dollars' worth of assets, and there's the guy who has made a million dollars in a year. That's a real privilege, but I never knew that it had happened and I didn't know it when it was over with. . .and then, I'm a crazy guy anyway because I've given so much of it away.

The accumulation of wealth for its own sake has never held any interest for me whatsoever. I enjoy life and I enjoy wealth for what it allows us to do in life.

I am sad that during the growth of the Gold Seal Company, I was away from home so much when my first wife was caring for our children. It's a kind of sorrow. I am sure that my being a success in the creation of the Gold Seal Company and whatever wealth I've created or any good I've done, were what cost me my first home. So that's a sure sign that my money couldn't buy happiness for me.

On the other hand, I live a happy life. I am a guy who enjoys life, and I enjoy participation in whatever I am doing — in fact, I am enjoying sitting here talking to you, Boyd. But I don't think money can make you happy.

We live in a funny world, though, where people seem to believe that they can buy happiness. There's an old philosophy somewhere that says, "It's not what you make; it's what you save." You can find all kinds of one-line philosophies to live by, I guess.

But happiness is an indescribable thing. What's happiness to you might not be happiness to me. I have some friends who work for me who don't want success particularly. They want a certain position in life and an association with certain people.

I have offered advancement to a few very nice people who work for me who don't want it and don't take it when their chance comes along. They say, "Just leave me right here. I'm happy and comfortable doing what I want to do." And if that's what really makes them happy, they've made the right decision, and they're successful, too, in their own way.

Roger Maris

I'm a fan of Roger Maris the baseball player. I don't claim to know Roger Maris the man. I've interviewed him on two occasions and found his candor and intelligent insights into his sport a refreshing departure from the time-worn cliches that sports are heir to.

I have the impression that Maris decided early on in his baseball career that he would let his exploits on the playing field speak for him. But, sadly, that was not good enough for the reporters who followed his heroic efforts in 1961, when Maris broke the most cherished record in baseball: sixty home runs, to beat the immortal Babe Ruth's single-season record by one.

Maris was hounded by the press corps when it became obvious he had a chance to break the record. A shy, introspective person, Maris was not prepared for the celebrity status he was suddenly forced to accept. And he wasn't prepared for the barrage of questions forced on him by an inquiring press that in many cases looked on him as a hunk of meat and muscle to simply be exploited.

One reporter asked, "Do you fool around on the road?" Another writer filed a so-called "exclusive interview" critical of Maris' attitude toward the media. The reporter had not talked with him.

Then there was the attitude of fans and writers alike that if anyone was going to break Ruth's record, it should be Roger's more popular teammate Mickey Mantle. Mantle finished that season with fifty-four home runs.

That was the atmosphere in which Maris operated as he pursued the record that people had said would never be broken.

A nervous disorder caused him to lose some of his hair. Maris took his meals alone in the privacy of his hotel room to escape the crush of reporters and fans who followed him everywhere off the field. Photographers trailed him from the dugout to the on-deck circle as he waited his turn at bat.

But through all the distractions Maris was able to marshall the skills that made him the league's Most Valuable Player on two occasions with the New York Yankees. And on the final day of the season, Boston's Tracy Stallard served up a pitch that Maris put into the right field seats — the record-setting home run.

It should have been a happy time for Roger Maris. But the 1961 season and the subsequent years in New York left some scars. Still wary of the press, Roger does now grant an occasional interview. "I'll give you one more chance," he says.

So here's Roger telling it as it was in 1961.

Roger, it's no secret you had differences of opinion with the media reporters covering you in that very turbulent year of 1961. Hank Greenberg, the former general manager of the Cleveland Indians who also had assaulted Babe Ruth's record in 1938 when he hit fifty-eight homers, had an interesting observation. He said, "The writers protected me then. Why aren't the protecting Maris now?"

How do you react to that?

I think I can see what he was talking about. There was no protection there whatsoever. You know, I was just an open piece of merchandise that everybody was picking at, trying to get something the most unusual.

Of course, I think I was right there at the era in which a lot of eager young writers were coming in. The other writers named them themselves; they called them "the chipmunks." They were trying to make names for themselves fast at anyone's expense, and unfortunately for myself, I happened to be that guy.

Roger Kahn, who authored the book **The Boys of Summer***, the story of the Dodgers of 1955, wrote some very nice things about you in 1961. He said, "Maris is being covered more intensely than any sports figure in history. He has to protect himself. But to do this he would have to duck questions and tell half-truths, and that's contrary to Roger's nature."*

You know, I have had a lot of time to think about this in all these twenty years that have gone past. And I always look at Howard Cosell. Howard believes in that saying, "Tell it like it is." That has sort of made Howard Cosell as a public figure.

Yet I think back to when I was doing all of this stuff, and I was telling it like it was, and I got in all kinds of trouble because nobody wanted to know the truth. All they wanted was prefabricated stories, or maybe some stuff that is just not my nature. When I was asked a question, I gave an answer.

Roger Kahn had another interesting quote. He said, "Maris' personality is unfinished." You were twenty-seven years old at the time and I don't know if anybody could have been prepared for what happened to you in 1961. He observed that and he wrote, "He will change."

Did you change at all before you left baseball? Obviously you have changed now, looking back in retrospect on what went on back then.

I think about the only change I can see that happened to me in baseball from the time I entered to the time I left is that they pushed me into somewhat of a shell, rather than being the easy-going person that I really was.

I think right back to all the years that I played ball, signing autographs, doing a lot of things around the ballpark after the games. I had to stop doing all that because it was no longer possible. I was no longer able to do it because of all the attention and the crowds that followed my every move.

At one time I could just come out of the ballpark and stand there for an hour, signing autographs, something like that. I did that when I was with Cleveland, Kansas City and even with New York in the early part of '61.

Then this thing just got so big and out of hand that it was virtually impossible to do some of that stuff. You start hiding more. It drove me more or less into a shell, and I just tried to stay away from everything.

And of course, with the writers on my back the way they were. . .the more they dogged me, the less I wanted to be out in front of them.

You also were asked, naturally, a lot of silly questions, some of them over and over. I was going to start this interview with one of the worst, and I have to work it in here someplace: "What would you rather do, hit sixty-one home runs or bat .300?"

That was one of the real winners that I was asked. Of course when I was asked that question, I asked the writer back, "Well, really, what would you rather do?"

And he said, "I'd rather bat .300."

And I said, "Well, to each his own." It just shows the mentality of the guy that's asking the question because, you know, how many guys hit .300 and how many hit sixty-one home runs? The first time in thirty-four years that anything like this had happened — you go back the last thirty-four years and tell me how many guys hit .300! And this yo yo is telling me that he would rather do that.

Ford Frick, the commissioner of baseball at the time, very arbitrarily ruled, when it was obvious that both you and Mickey Mantle had a good shot at Babe's single season record, that it had to be done within the framework of one hundred fifty-four games. You, of course, were playing a one hundred sixty-two game schedule that season.

How did that affect you — how did you react to that, Roger?

It really didn't bother me. I didn't really care what Ford Frick said.

When he made the ruling, it was like letting the horse out of the barn and then going to close the gate. You should make a ruling like that before someone does something, not afterwards. That was my contention right from the start, even before I thought I had a shot at anything.

We were asked that question, Mickey and myself, and my contention was if somebody does hit it, I think that they deserve to keep it...which I thought that they did, and I still think they do, and it doesn't bother me one way or the other if there is an asterisk there in the record book or not.

When I look at when I hit my last home run, I hit it in my own hundred fifty-first ballgame, so if he wants to do this thing, let's do it from first to last. I hit my first one in the eleventh game of the season.

That's right. You missed one game with an injury, and you took yourself out late in the season.

Right, so there are one hundred fifty-one games. Actually, one hundred sixty-three games were played that year because of a rain-out at one time, I think. Then I sat out one and was pulled out of another in the first inning because they put some eyedrops in my eyes and they dilated my pupils, so I got an official game counted that time when I hadn't even gotten up to bat.

Reggie Jackson made an interesting statement, I think, in about 1977. He said, "Roger Maris had to act that way to keep his sanity." And he went on to say, "People don't know what Roger went through in 1961." Then he added, "For someone to do what Maris did in 1961, he would have to be deaf and dumb."

Pretty strong words! In other words, Jackson had some great empathy for you; he had some idea of what you had gone through in '61.

He got a little bit of a taste in New York.

If you have to play sports, I guess there could be no better place to play than in New York if you are trying to do something, make a name for yourself. And on the other hand, it can probably be the cruelest place to play, depending on which side of the fence you are on, and unfortunately my side was not too good. And Reggie has had somewhat of a taste of some of that in New York.

It gets very difficult to maintain your sanity. Very difficult.

During spring training in 1963, you more or less boycotted the press for awhile, didn't you?

Oh, I might have. I don't know.

A writer wrote that it got to the point where his colleagues were saying, "If he's not going to talk to us, the hell with him. So we kind of left him alone after that."

They might have said that. But they really didn't mean it, because they kept bothering me. I felt like leaving them totally alone. I probably did and was hoping they would leave me alone, but they would still come around. You know, you get tired of people asking you such stupid things.

When you haven't done anything and you aren't doing anything, what news are you anyway?

What obligation does a pro athlete have to the media, Roger?

Personally, I don't feel you have any, as long as they aren't going to write what you say with any sort of accuracy. And this was a problem I was having, not with all of them, but with most of them.

They would want an interview with you, and you would give them the interview. Then you would read the story and it would be completely different.

If I had had somebody sitting there as a witness or tape-recorded the interview, and then compared that version with the printed interview, the two wouldn't even coincide. All it did when they were interviewing me was to give them the privilege of saying, "I interviewed Maris," and they were accurate just up to that point in saying it. But what I actually said never seemed to show up in print.

*You told a **Newsweek** reporter, Roger, in 1976, "I found the less people know about you, the better off you are. The press usually wants to talk about sour grapes, and I don't have anything to be sour about." It sounded like you had mellowed a little bit there.*

No. I'll tell you what it is. Every time someone comes for an interview, and this goes right up to the present time today, and I can give him an interview, I'll say, "OK, I'll try you again." What invariably happens is that the very first thing you see when you read the guy's article is, "Maris is still bitter, Maris is still sour, Maris is still this or that."

I'm not bitter about nothing. I was never bitter about nothing. The only thing I don't like is that I don't like to be quoted wrong. Say what I say, then I'll be happy about it. But don't go and write something in there that I didn't say, so that I'll come back to you and ask, "How can you put stuff in there like that?"

Well, it makes better copy. But I don't care about his copy. I want what I said, said.

I think a good example of that was when one reporter asked you who your favorite male singer was. You answered, "Frank Sinatra." Then he asked you who your favorite female singer was, and you said, "I don't have one."

And what did the guy say? "Is it OK if I write down Doris Day?"

Yeah, there it was, you know. They prefabricate all the time. They do what they want to do. This was when I said, "You guys write what you want to write and you know what you've got in mind, what you want me to say, before you ever ask me a question." So consequently, if I don't answer their questions properly, they are going to put what they want in there anyway.

So why even bother me?

In researching this interview, I found there has only been one book written on what you accomplished in 1961; you wrote that with reporter Jim Ogle. But there hasn't really been a good book written about your experiences of what you went through that year. That story never really has been told.

No, it really hasn't been, and I don't know if I'd really want to write it.

I look at all this stuff — well, you know, not everyone can be a Jim Bouton where you're just a gossip columnist, and write the garbage that he wrote and try to make some money off of it.

I don't think anyone is really interested in what actually happened to me in those years. Nobody knows the hardships I went through. Nobody can tell — I can't even sit here and tell you just what this experience did to me. And so for me to try to relate it in a book and come out with something, I can't really see it happening.

A manager or a wheeler-dealer of some kind said, "If Mantle or Maris breaks Ruth's record, it could be worth a half a million dollars for a life story or maybe a movie." Did they ever seriously consider a movie about you? Was that ever talked about?

No, nothing like that happened, though I don't know what I would have done if it had. I'm not really interested in a lot of that stuff.

The press in many of those years was always saying that all I was, was money-hungry, that all I cared about was money. But yet I am probably the guy who has gotten the least money for doing what I did of everybody who's broken a record like that. I bet you Pete Rose capitalized more on his forty-four straight hits than I did on my sixty-one.

It's just that it really didn't mean that much to me. Sure, I wanted to make money. But there were a lot of things I turned down and a lot of places I didn't go because I just didn't want to do those things.

Something that kept popping up in a lot of things I read about you, Roger, was the statement that you were very concerned about building security for your family. Obviously a baseball player doesn't know how many years he has. But that came up time after time: "I'm interested in some security for my family." That was a prime concern of yours, obviously.

That was the only concern I had, as far as baseball or anything else is concerned. I think any ball player or any athlete who enters pro sports thinks at one time or another that his bubble is not going to burst. I have news for him. You have to look at it in terms of security.

I recently saw an article in a baseball magazine titled "Where Are They Now?" You read about this guy being a pipefitter and that guy being a cowboy on some ranch. I didn't want to end up in that category. And I didn't wind up there only because of the way I did think ahead.

Speaking of that, that takes us to your move to St. Louis in 1967 and 1968. That turned out to be an excellent move for you, obviously, and a very happy move.

It was a good move. Of course, I didn't want to go there at first. I really had no intentions of playing that following year until the Yankees traded me.

This was another real courtesy shot that the Yankees gave me. When I told them in July of '66 that I was not going to play in '67, they went and traded me even up for Charley Smith.

I had some thinking to do because I had to figure if I wanted to go ahead with more bad press. They'd have said, "Well, because he was traded from the Yankees, he quit." So that's the only reason I went ahead and played in St. Louis in '67.

Is it safe to say that you were happy those two years in St. Louis?

Oh, yes. I was very happy. St. Louis is a good place to play. I was playing with great people. And I ended up playing on two great ball clubs.

The only problem was that I felt that I was finished. I broke my hand in '65, and after that, I lost my strength in the two lower fingers on that hand. I couldn't swing the bat the same way.

Your relationship with the St. Louis Cardinals opened up what was a pretty nice business opportunity, the Budweiser beer distributorship in Gainesville, Florida. I have heard varying accounts of that. Was it a gift from Mr. Busch for playing with the Cardinals? Did he approve you for this?

If it was a gift, he owes me some money!

No, basically what happened is this. The toughest part is to get the brewery's approval to buy one. I did buy it and, fortunately, by my being there in St. Louis I did get the approval of Mr. Busch, which was the opportunity that I probably needed.

I heard a rumor in Fargo in the late '60s, about the time you were retiring, that you were looking to buy a business and settle back in your old home town. Did that ever cross you mind?

Yes, I was thinking about that at that time. But you have to go where your opportunities go and I didn't think I really had the opportunities there in Fargo. I never did get back. There were a few things we had looked into and just nothing materialized.

Much was made, when the press started retracing your entire life almost back to the crib in 1961, of the fact that you and your brother Rudy changed schools as teen-agers. I think the point was that "Roger Maris had been petulant from the time that he was a young boy" — that you didn't like Central High School so you switched to Fargo Shanley. What really happened that year?

You understand the old high school politics, I think — sports politics. You know, there are a lot of politics in sports, both pro and high school. I see it right back where I am at now with my own children.

Rudy and I were playing sports at Fargo Central. It all came about over football. Rudy was playing for one coach, and the following year another coach took over there. This guy wanted for some reason to shelve us. We figured, "Well, if we aren't good enough to play there, we are good enough to play somewhere else" — somewhere where you can go and win the state championship rather than sit around floundering with this other guy.

That's about what it amounted to, going over to Sid Cichy at Shanley. Rudy and I fit in very well in their backfield. It turned out very well.

You played for Sid for, what, two or three years?

I played for Sid two years.

Sid just retired a couple years ago. People believe he has become a legend in his own time in Fargo. Obviously he was a little ahead of his time even in the '50s when you were around.

He had a great record and had a great rapport with the kids who worked for him. He worked hard for them, too. He was a great coach and his record speaks for itself.

*You told a reporter for **Time Magazine** once, "I'd have played college football if I had been smart enough to get into school." You thought of going to Oklahoma to play football, didn't you, Rog?*

Yeah, I went down. I came close to going to Oklahoma. I just really didn't like the school. I guess I wasn't ready for the academic part of it, and with the baseball option hanging there, I just went into baseball instead.

Did a guy from the Chicago Cubs really tell you, "Don't play baseball, son. You're too small. You'll never make it"?

Yeah. I worked out with the Cubs before Cleveland in 1952. I spent a week in Chicago working out with them. The final advice I got was, "You might as well forget baseball; you're too small." That's just one man's opinion anyway.

As we're talking now, the nation is waiting out a baseball strike. What's your reaction on what's happening in baseball, as we record this in the middle of June, 1981?

I guess, being an ex-baseball player, naturally you believe that if you were still playing, you would be right with the baseball players and doing what they are doing.

But you know, the ball players for a good number of years — however long Marvin Miller has been around, eighteen years or so — they have come a long way. They have gotten a lot of things. The salaries have gotten awful high. The benefits have all been good. The owners now are in a predicament where they have to get some compensation for the good players they are losing. If they don't, I think they are in trouble, so I can understand their side of it, too. Just being in business, I can understand their way of thinking.

I think they are going to hold out for quite awhile, because they are at a point where they see they have to make a move.

Speaking of the owners and management, did you ever go back for Old-Timers Day at Yankee Stadium?

Yeah, I have gone — oh, I guess maybe the last four years.

There were a number of years, then, when you maybe decided you didn't want to go back for awhile?

Well, I didn't go back for about ten years after I quit playing. I just didn't really feel I was an old-timer. I really didn't want to get involved in that. I don't know. I had had it up over my head with baseball at that point. And I didn't want to get back with it. I knew one day I would; it was just a question of when.

Mentally, I think, you have to be ready to go back, especially someone in my position, because baseball could have been a lot better for me than it really was.

I have a lot of great memories with it, and I also have a lot of bad memories. I had to sort of pick and choose when I was ready to go back.

You have been ignored by the writers as far as the Hall of Fame is concerned. Let me ask you — do you feel your performance in your twelve years in the major leagues was good enough to warrant your entry into the Baseball Hall of Fame?

You asking for a personal opinion?

Yeah, a personal opinion.

Well, as a personal opinion, then: I think it was. But it doesn't bother me that I am not in there. I think every ball player, when he starts out in baseball, dreams of maybe doing something that will get him into the Hall of Fame. But circumstances turn out different for some of us.

I really don't care now. It doesn't make any difference one way or another anymore. I feel that the way baseball has been with my record — they have not done justice to some of the things I have accomplished anyway, so consequently, how can I expect anything out of them?

One thing that keeps coming through — there still seem to be some loose ends. I mentioned earlier that the 1961 season was never really chronicled in a good book about you, that you probably didn't receive a lot of the recognition that you deserved, and you really didn't cash in on that as well as you could have. Now, this Hall of Fame thing...do you know what I am getting at?

There seem to be a lot of loose ends in your career as yet. Do you look at it that way too?

No, I really don't care because it's all past.

You know, I see kids come up to me, and I see people come up to me who were kids in my era of playing. They are all thrilled and excited to see me, even now. It's gratifying to see that these people still care.

I couldn't care less about baseball itself or what the writers themselves think in terms of what has happened with me in '61, whether I deserve it or don't deserve it or what.

You know, it's really pretty much immaterial.

I have asked this question Roger, of other famous fathers who have named one of their sons "Junior." You have a Roger Maris, Jr. Does that present any problems for your son?

Yeah. It creates a lot of them. I think that's probably one of the dumbest things for people to do, naming their kids after themselves!

How does it affect Roger, Jr.?

In many respects. He has always got to be on his best behavior. He's not supposed to do this or that simply because he is Roger Maris, Junior. It's like I always tell him: "You know, you can look at your name and it can go two ways. It can either go good for you or it can go bad for you."

You have a certain number of people who are sort of thrilled when they hear it and say, "You're Roger's son," and are really happy to meet him. On the other hand, others mutter "that no-good you-know-what," and they make it harder on him. It's probably a fifty-fifty deal.

Roger, we had a conversation in Fargo about '65, in which I asked you what you might like to do when you got out of baseball. You probably don't remember the answer. You said, "I'd kinda like to get in the business you're in, because sportscasting looks attractive."

Did you ever think any more about that?

I tell you, Boyd: I might have thought it was attractive in those days, but the experience of hitting sixty-one home runs took away all of its attractions for me.

There were a lot of things I thought I would like to do. I thought that one day when my career was over with, I really would have liked to stick around as a third base coach or a first base coach in baseball — I wouldn't want to be a manager. I always thought it would be nice to just stick around in baseball. But because of the turn of events, in those circumstances I really wouldn't care to do it.

I have some good friends right now managing in baseball, and a lot of times I think it would be nice going back with these guys. I really don't know, though, if I could hack that grind. Someday I may try it for a year, just to see — that, I really don't know.

As for your business here, this broadcasting: you know, it looks like a good busniess to go into. A lot of ball players are making good money at it. And all you have to do is talk to do it, you know — just be able to talk. It probably looks a lot more glamorous than it really is, though.

But it's not the glamour I want, just something to do. And I have enough to do with Budweiser nowadays that I really don't need any more headaches.

Hey, we got the word "Budweiser" in, and that's a good note to end on. Good seeing you, Roger.

Good seeing you again, too, Boyd.

The Baseball Writers of America vote each year on entrants to baseball's prestigious Hall of Fame. The Hall is reserved for baseball's elite, the super-stars and the record-setters.

Does Roger Maris warrant a spot among baseball's best? I think he does. But the writers who dubbed him "uncooperative," "sullen" and "petulant" more than twenty years ago haven't forgiven him yet.

Roger Maris was willing to let his exploits on the field say all that needed to be said about him. I think the message was loud and clear.

Quentin Burdick

"If at first you don't succeed. . . ." That phrase could have been coined by U.S. Senator Quentin Burdick, whose illustrious career in North Dakota's congressional delegation began with trying again, and again, and again, and again.

Between 1934 and 1958 Burdick sought public office six times, and six times he was defeated.

But his tenacity paid off twenty-five years ago. The voters of North Dakota began electing him, and have kept him in Washington ever since, two of those years in the House of Representatives and the rest in the Senate. His current term, for which he was already campaigning at the time of this interview in 1980, expires in 1988.

People always remember the victories in politics. But your great win over John Davis in 1960 and your election to the House in 1958 were preceded by some rather lean years politically, weren't they?

Yes, first came five or six races in which I didn't get the most votes.

Let's start with the first time you went after an elective office. When was that?

That was back in 1934 when I ran against A.R. Bergesen, a very popular state's attorney in Cass County. And of course he defeated me.

Then I ran against his assistant, and he defeated me. Then I ran against Art Fowler for state senator and he defeated me. Then I ran for lieutenant governor against Oscar Hagen.

Was that in 1938?

Yes, and we were defeated.
Then I ran for governor in 1946, and I was defeated.

By Fred G. Aandahl.

That's right.

So now...

Now, just a minute, Boyd — there's one more. I ran against Milt Young in 1956 and was defeated.

OK, now between 1946 and 1956 there was a ten-year lapse in your political activity. Were you practicing law then?

Mostly, yes.

And then in 1958 you were elected to the U.S. House of Representatives. That was your first elective victory, wasn't it?

That is right.

After all those years, was the campaign in 1958 going to be, maybe, the "last hurrah" for you? Can we look at it in those terms? What might have happened, had you not won?

Well, based upon my history, I would have had to run again.

Now, you only served a year in the House, 1959.

Well, a year and a few months.

Then you had that great race in 1960 — I think, one of the great races in North Dakota political history — against John Davis to fill the unexpired term of the late U.S. Senator Bill Langer.

What bothered me about that race was that it was held in June — primary time. I wouldn't have been much afraid of that race in the fall but I was afraid of it in June, because no one votes for a Democrat in June.

Why do you say that?

Well, they just didn't in those days. They only turned out in the fall.

It required a lot of effort, and I worked quite hard in that campaign, I will tell you!

Let's talk about that campaign in 1960. What were the issues that were being discussed in North Dakota in 1960?

Oh, about the same issues that have been discussed for years and years. It's always mainly agriculture — who could do the best job for the farmers on the agriculture front.

At that time the U.S. Secretary of Agriculture, Ezra Taft Benson, wasn't doing so well. The slogan was "beat Burdick with Benson." You see, it was farm issues, same as always.

You went to bed that night not knowing if you had won the election or not.

That's right. I went to bed two nights without knowing!

It was a long span, anyway, with you waiting for the results from a small little area in the western part of the state.

A small little area known as the Indian reservation, where they took their time bringing in the ballots.

And your margin of victory ended up about eleven hundred votes.

Eleven hundred and eighty-one.

What were your thoughts for those two days? How would you describe those moments of waiting?

It was just like waiting for a jury to come in — very difficult, very difficult. You don't know which way it's going to go, and you plan in both directions...especially what's going to happen if you are defeated again. You don't have to plan to be elected. But it's trying.

Did your political future flash before your eyes, after all the defeats you had suffered and the very close race that year?

Well, of course, it had been flashing for five or six times before that!

You replaced a North Dakota legend named William Langer.

I did.

What was your relationship with Wild Bill?

Very friendly. I have learned a lot from Bill Langer.

It began in 1932, when I graduated from the University of Minnesota and immediately plunged into politics with the Nonpartisan League. He was the most memorable politician I ever met — no doubt about it.

That man was a master as a politician. An absolute master! Let me give you one example that many people have heard about to show you how he had the personal touch.

He would drive all across the country by himself, and when he would get into an area at midnight he might decide to drive off the road and see some old farmer friend of his, Joe, up the line a ways. He would rap on the door, and Joe would come to the door and answer it in sleepy fashion. Mr. Langer would say, "I want to stay here."

Joe says, "Well, I only have one bed." Wild Bill says, "Just move over."

Langer slept with Joe all night. And the politics is this: That fellow Joe would talk about Langer sleeping with him for the next forty years. He would never quit.

Politics does make interesting bedfellows.

That's the kind of campaigner Bill Langer was. And you know, he did a lot of personal favors during the second World War. He was noted for breaking through the red tape and getting tractors for farmers, and so forth. He did a lot of personal things. . .and people just liked him.

History has been pretty kind to Bill Langer.

Yes, I think it has.

That might have surprised many of his contemporaries at the time who watched him involved in situations like his calling out the National Guard during the Depression. . .

He even made wild statements such as that you should shoot a fellow, a bank officer, like he was a chicken thief if he came to foreclose your farm on you. He had a perfect right to foreclose, of course, but that was the times — tough times, Dust Bowl times. They understood the language.

Did you ever ride the section lines campaigning with Bill Langer?

Did I!

I remember one time in Leonard when he showed up late. Mr. Langer liked everybody to be prompt at political meetings. He would walk into a meeting and they would all throw their hats in the air. Here I was, this eager young lawyer just out here in my first campaign holding a meeting for him in that little town, and that was the time he was late.

He was supposed to be there at two o'clock, so I got up and started talking shortly before then to hold the crowd. But you know, Boyd, he didn't show up until three o'clock.

What did you say?

I talked about the weather, I talked about the crops, I talked about football — I talked about everything. I would look into the crack of the door every few minutes: Where's Langer? He kept me there for three hours and then laughed about it.

Maybe that led to the early downfall of some of your campaigns. Maybe some people said, "Gee, Mr. Burdick didn't seem to be prepared at all for that speech!"

I talked about absolutely everything, I will tell you that!

What were campaigns like? Now, this was pre-television, and only a little radio was used. It was mainly hitting the stump and shaking hands, wasn't it?

Yes, and people came out for meetings. Now they don't come out quite so much. They have got the information without making the effort. It's easy for them — all they have to do is look at the tube.

In those days, you'd drive from city to city, from town hall to town hall. In your campaigns in the 1960s and 1970s, the rule is very slick television campaigns.

Well, "slick" is your word, Boyd. We try to get the message across the best we can in our own language.

Some people thought, for example, that Tom Kleppe's campaign for the House of Representatives was too slick. In looking back, I've heard many North Dakotans say that it just didn't fit the North Dakota style. It was too much Madison Avenue, too East Coast. Would you agree with that today?

There were certainly some errors to it.

Now, for example, one of the things in North Dakota that I learned long ago: don't bring in somebody else to talk for you. Talk for yourself. North Dakotans don't want anybody telling them who to vote for.

I would never have anybody come in for me; I never have had. We have invited some headliners to come in for fundraisers and so forth, but not here to talk for me, because I know those people out there. If you can't speak for yourself, set up on your hind legs and tell them what you think, who else is going to do it for you?

In politics, some names have their own legacy. Look at the Kennedy name. Now, Burdick has been a big name in North

Dakota politics for many years, first with Usher Burdick, then Quentin Burdick. Many people would assume that with a name like Burdick, you would almost have instant political success. But obviously it didn't work that way.

But you see, in those early years of running, I had a little bit of a handicap too because of my name.

There is some resentment against two members of one family on the ballot. Remember that when I was running for governor, my father was Congressman, and so forth. Some people resented it a little bit.

You notice that, the first time when I won, it was the first time when my father's name wasn't in the air — when he wasn't on the ticket in some way. That was in 1958 when I won.

But of course, all those years of losses established a foundation for me. I made friends and got to be known, so they weren't really losses. They were building a future.

What's the best political advice you ever got from your father? And I am sure there's a lot of it.

Oh, he gave me lots of advice. He said, "Just be yourself. Be humble, be yourself. Don't go for the slickness." That's what I recall. I think that advice of his still sells in North Dakota.

One of your favorite stories, one I've heard you tell at banquets on a couple of occasions, is a football story of your father's. I think it's worth retelling here.

Well, you know, he was tall on stories. I can't vouch for the veracity of all of them. But this one he claims is true.

He played football at the University of Minnesota when he was going to law school back around the turn of the century — 1902, 1903, something like that. Minnesota was playing Nebraska. In those days you didn't have these fancy bleachers like we have around here now, and the spectators would walk up and down the sidelines following the team, like they do on high school fields in some places. They didn't have fancy uniforms, either; in fact, they were pretty much the same.

It was getting toward dusk and Minnesota was ahead, but Nebraska was charging down the field. There were only a few minutes left but if they kept making five or six yards at a clip, Nebraska would have scored and beat Minnesota.

Well, Minnesota won. The Minneapolis Tribune came out the next day with the story of how Usher Burdick broke through, tackled their quarterback for a fifteen yard loss, and saved the game. Now, my father said with all that melee around there, with the dusk approaching and everybody excited, he simply lined up with the Nebraska team. The ball was snapped; and he turned around and nabbed the quarterback.

Whether it's true or not, it's a good story.

Well, he did nab the quarterback.

Let's shift gears. I talked with a former aide of yours at a press conference some years ago shortly after he had gone to work for you. I said, "How do you like Washington and what's it like working for a United States Senator?"

He said, "Let me tell you, traveling with this Burdick is something else." He said, "We both share the same motel room. We eat hamburgers a lot, and if there's any chance that we can drive across the state and get home and save having to get a motel room, he will do it." He added, "I sometimes think he thinks he is spending his own money."

Now, is that a press agent's dream for a public official, or is that how you really do travel on the road?

That's a product of the 1930s. It is. Anybody that has lived in the 1930s isn't going to waste any money. Those were tough days, and I suppose that's just ingrained in me. And I will admit that I am not too liberal with my spending.

Weren't you once voted one of the worst-dressed members of the United States Senate? I saw it in print.

No, no. . .second.

You were second?

I was beaten by a multi-millionaire, Claiborne Pell.

What was your reaction? Or better yet, what was your wife Jocelyn's reaction when she saw that? What did she say?

She smiled a bit.

I presume I was just coming in on one of the flights from North Dakota and walked into the Senate chamber when they caught me.

Did Jocie start picking out your ties or anything after that?

Yes, she has been a little more careful. But Claiborne beating me — a multi-millionaire from Rhode Island. Imagine that!

Of course, you say you are used to finishing second in competition. That shouldn't have bothered you at all, being second worst dressed!

You mentioned a millionaire. . .there are now nineteen, I have read, in the United States Senate. What does that suggest about obtaining higher office in our country? Do you have to have a lot of money of your own, a big fat personal bank account, to be elected to the United States Senate?

I presume that money helps in some states but, as we have seen in North Dakota, the big spenders don't necessarily win.

Of course, it takes money in this modern age. We've talked about television; you know the cost of it. People are getting used to the amount of money it takes. You must have some friends; you must have some money. You just can't go out with a very low budget like we used to and expect to win a campaign.

Do you realize that I ran for Congress on a budget of $2,800?

That was in 1958?

Yes. I had my own signs. You know, those up-and-down signs you see on telephone booths — I inaugurated them. And I had the hammer and nails in the back end of my old car, an old Reo. I put up most of them myself.

And not only that. . .have you seen reversed black ads, with type showing up on a solid black background? I mean the one-column ads, just little ones. I started them by buying a couple of pages, you know — one column by an inch on each page.

This is a poor man's campaign.

Campaigns have gotten longer, haven't they?

Yes, and I think six weeks or maybe two months are plenty long enough to campaign. If you can't sell yourself and your program in that period of time, you will never sell it.

What has drawn the campaigns out so long?

I don't know. I suppose it's the man who wants to get in but is not in. He thinks a long lead and an early start might be helpful. I don't know whether that's correct or not.

You will stand for reelection in 1982. You will be seventy-four years old then. Is that right?

Well, I will be seventy-four during the year, yes.

If you are reelected and serve out that term, you will be eighty years old by the time you leave the Senate. Is that too old? Some people think our senators sometimes hang on too long, you know.

We occasionally hear people say, "Why, after they have served for so long, don't they step down and take a rest and give a younger guy a shot?" Is that a fair criticism, if in fact it is a criticism?

It really is. But you remember, it all depends on a man's physical and mental awareness. If he is physically strong, mentally alert and awake, I don't know why years should make that difference.

Should we have gotten rid of some of our great leaders in the world like Churchill? Should we have gotten rid of a lot of our great minds in the Supreme Court?

It all depends upon the individual. Some people are old at fifty. Some people aren't old at eighty. So it's just a question of the individual.

How about in party politics? Say, for example, you have a senator who is seventy-five or eighty years old. Is pressure ever brought to bear on the incumbent? Do they occasionally say, "Hey, you have had your turn in there — let's give someone else a chance"?

Oh, I suppose it has happened, but I have no great knowledge of it. You know, the incumbent is generally by that time in a very fine position to help his state.

And you talk about seniority — that isn't everything, but with it you get on the Appropriations Committee or on the Agriculture Committee, where at the same time a younger man just starting out would take maybe fifteen, twenty years to reach the same point. You have to measure that into the equation, too, you know, because that vote on the committee can be very, very important for this state or any small state.

You mentioned seniority. . .the seniority system sometimes comes under attack. How do you feel about that criticism of it?

I recognize that there are some shortcomings about the system. But every time you mention that, you have to talk about an alternative that would improve on it. And I don't know of one that would work better.

For example, take getting your room assignment in the office buildings in Washington. Shouldn't the older men have a choice? They have been there longer; they have tended the fires all these years.

What other systems would you use? Most people don't seem to realize that every time it is exercised, you have to take a vote. We haven't got the seniority system automatically now; we have to vote it. Every man is made a member of a committee, or a chairman of the committee, after they have a vote at the Senate. The seniority system may be there, but it has to be re-voted and supported and confirmed each time, not only by a caucus of the two parties, but also by the Senate as a whole.

So there are safeguards against its abuse built into the system. If you've got a bad chairman, for example, you can get rid of him.

Is it nervous time in Congress when senators and representatives vote on their pay raises? That must be a difficult situation.

It is an absolutely calm time for me. My father never voted for a raise and I never have, either. That is just the way I feel about it.

Now, there are so many things that go with the job besides salary. There's honor, and there's prestige. No one is there just for the money.

People with families do have troubles, I know. But I knew what the salary was when I went out there, and they did too.

What was your salary when you went in 1960?

I am trying to think. . .somewhere in the twenties or low thirties, as I recall.

What is it now — $57,000 or $58,000?

Yes, plus the fringe benefits. I think it's about sixty now, because this last raise went into effect.

Have you maintained a home in Washington since 1960?

A permanent home? No, I have lived in an apartment. Never a home.

Haven't you ever had your family with you in Washington?

My wife now spends four or five months with me in the early part of the year. She comes home for the summer months and then I commute in the fall a little.

Are there many senators who bring their families with them to Washington?

I would say most of them do. Very few of them have conducted it the way I have done.

I have done a lot of traveling, of course. At the same time I make an appearance for some group of people or on some program in North Dakota, I always come home for awhile.

This is probably a difficult question because I am assuming that you have had many — but is there a proud moment or two that stand out in your career? Something that you have done politically that you are especially proud of?

I think that when it's all said and done, when it's all over, I think the part that I played in bringing the two-party system to the state will probably give me a great deal of pleasure.

We were in disarray until we got two parties in North Dakota. . .not that there's anything wrong with even more parties, but having two parties brings order. There's responsibility on the party that's in power to deliver, and it's the responsibility of the party that's out to show why the party that's in should be out.

It was about 1956, as I recall, when Ray Vendsel stood up at the national Democratic convention to say, "From the United States' newest two-party state" as he cast his vote.

Yes, it was 1956 when we made the switch of the Nonpartisan League into the Democratic Party. I was the first candidate for the Senate at that time running under this new banner of the combined forces of Democrats and Leaguers.

See, the League was a product of the agrarian movement years ago. It never was a political party. The Farmer-Labor Party was a part of that agrarian movement, and the progressives like LaFollette were part of it. All of them found a home within the Democratic column, but none of them, for various reasons, liked to make the switch.

My father never made the switch, nor did Bill Langer. They had been in the Republican column for years and years and years before the parting of the ways. That didn't make them any less progressive or any more progressive. They just felt that was historically where they should be.

Some people in the electorate had the impression that you had changed parties in 1958 when you ran for the House as the Democratic-NPL candidate. Isn't that correct?

I know I have heard that statement. But it really wasn't changing parties at all, because I was a member of the Nonpartisan League, and the Nonpartisan League each year would vote for it's own candidates. And they generally voted in the Republican Party because that's where they had been. But there was nothing to prevent them from following in the Democratic column.

So you had a Republican and a Democratic Party, but you really had a Nonpartisan League political association. That's what I was a member of.

Why, sure, I ran for lieutenant governor, you might say, as a Republican. But I really ran as the Nonpartisan Leaguer.

Was that the big factor in making North Dakota a solid two-party state? I imagine many, many things contributed, but what were some of the things that may have been a part of that, Senator?

I think, first of all, the growing feeling that so many of our programs were coming from Washington. There had to be political identification with them.

For example, the Roosevelt period — for the many years he was in office, he was associated with farm programs and water programs and so forth. There became a national association with the Democratic Party that you didn't have with your little third party ballots.

I think that's what crystallized it.

Let's go back and swap another story. I am going to mention a case to you that's going to ring a bell — Haug versus Grimm, 1957. One of our spies gave me this information. This was in your days as trial lawyer, and you butted heads with another former guest on this program, Judge Ronald Davies, in a personal injury suit.

I am very well acquainted with it!

I know it's one of your favorite stories. What happened in that case?

Ron Davies was and is a very good friend of mine. But you know, when a friend assumes the robes and takes the bench, a lawyer always stands back out of the way — he doesn't want to be in the position of influencing the judge through friendship. And that's one of the bad things about being a judge, that you become immediately disassociated with many of your friends who are lawyers.

Well, when Ron was new on the bench, we had a case up in Grand Forks where I was defending the driver of a car, and I belive Martin Vogel was representing the plaintiff. . .

The passenger in the car.

Yes, who was bringing a "passenger suit," as we call it. You had to prove gross negligence at the time.

Vogel won, and I took an appeal up on the grounds that Judge Davies — my friend and my fraternity brother and legal colleague — had erroneously instructed the jury to my damage.

Now bear in mind, he had just been appointed to the bench a few months ago. This was the first appeal to the Circuit Court of Appeals in St. Louis. . .and I beat him.

Every time we meet we snicker about that one.

Every now and then we hear someone use the word "government" almost like a swear word. How do you feel about that attitude which some people — a lot of people, quite frankly — have toward our government?

It's unfortunate. It's too bad, because the government is the people, and the people can change the government, can make the government any way they want it. They've got the power of the ballot box, a power that people don't have in many parts of the world. So when they talk about the government, they're really taking about themselves.

This is a democratic form of government in which everyone has a vote. If they just sit around and complain and don't do anything about it — don't act and don't vote — they are going to get the kind of government they deserve.

The opportunities were there for you when you were starting out in politics, though obviously you were unsuccessful in many early campaigns before you were elected. Are they still available for young politicians today, starting out on the route that you chose?

Certainly! Absolutely! The gates are wide open. They can do it.

They just have to have the stick-to-it-iveness to stay with it, that's all.

Of course they can. And many have done it.

I can't let you go without asking you this one question: Are you entertaining any thoughts about your seeking re-election in 1982?

Of course I am.

As long as I am vigorous. . .as long as I maintain the good mental state that I think I do. . .why, of course I am going to run. I am going to run because I think I can still deliver for the state of North Dakota in many capacities that a new man couldn't.

Will you be looking at the same issues in 1982 that we're looking at now, in 1980?

Ever since I have been in politics, we have always had the farm question. In the last two years now, a new question has been injected into the campaign, and that's going to be energy.

Of course, North Dakota is right in the eye of the needle. With its lignite and its oil and with its gas and with its water, we will be right in the middle of energy considerations as well as the agriculture situation.

I think North Dakota has a very, very exciting future ahead of it.

Dr. Anne Carlsen

Dr. Anne Carlsen game me a hearty wave as she pulled her car into the parking lot adjacent to Prairie Public TV's studio in Fargo. I was going to talk with her about the realities of life as a physically handicapped person in a world that sometimes unconsciously erects barriers. I was about to see one such barrier demonstrated.

Dr. Anne describes her condition as "quadruple congenital amputation." She was born without arms from the elbows down. The one leg with which she was born was deformed from its knee down and was amputated when she was fifteen. She manuevers well with crutches, but steps — particularly high steps — can present a problem. And there were two extremely high steps between her and the back door of our studio.

I was embarrassed. How could I have overlooked this problem? Dr. Anne saw my frustration but reacted with practicality. "There's a small suitcase in the trunk of my car," she told me. "Put it below the first step, and maybe I can make it up from there.

"If that doesn't work, we may have to do our interview out here!"

I managed a nervous laugh. With some tugging, pulling and lifting, and with the assistance of her suitcase, I managed to assist her through the back door...only to see the whole scene repeated inside as we encountered the raised platform that held the set for our interview.

When she was finally seated in her chair I said, "Well, Dr. Anne, I think the hardest part of this interview is over." We both laughed. And we laughed even harder when it really was over — and we discovered a special ramp for the handicapped located around the corner of the building. I had never known it existed.

Later I would recall that while Dr. Anne's handicap is obvious at first glance, there are other equally serious handicaps which are not...like ignorance of the needs and lifestyles of people around you.

"The Anne Carlsen School for the Physically Handicapped" — that's the new name for the well-known Crippled Children's School at Jamestown, North Dakota, just renamed in honor of the woman who's committed her life to it. Dr. Anne, as she's affectionately known among her friends and students, has been the administrator for thirty years.

You have actually been involved with the school since its beginning in 1941, isn't that right? Almost forty years, then.

That's right.

I was very pleased to see the new name that has been added, the Anne Carlsen School. How do you feel about having a respected school like this named after you? That's pretty heavy stuff, isn't it?

That it is indeed! It's an honor. It's a little embarrassing, though, and it seems kind of strange when I see that school bus running around town with my name on it.

But I think that some of the youngsters are glad to get the old name dropped — the Crippled Children's School — although it did tell specifically what we deal with.

That's been something that makes people uncomfortable, the names we use to describe the handicapped. "Crippled" has always seemed like such a harsh word.

It is a harsh word. Of course it's a harsh condition, too.

How do we describe your handicap, then, in the correct terminology?

The medical diagnosis would be "quadruple congenital amputation." It means that when I was born, I was without arms from the elbows down. I did have one leg, but it was deformed from the knee down and was amputated when I was fifteen. In layman's terms, I guess you would say I am without arms and legs, maybe.

But you are blessed with a great sense of humor. I read an interview you gave to a reporter in Evansville, Indiana, in which you mentioned that you do have trouble with zippers.

That I do. . .if they are on the side. I can do them if they are on the back or on the front.

Tell us about your family, the Carlsen family back in Wisconsin.

My parents both came from Denmark. My dad, Alfred Carlsen, came over to America when he was about twenty-seven because of economic conditions. He was a florist. When he first came to this country, he worked in a florist shop in the Twin Cities, and then moved to Grantsburg, Wisconsin, and bought a farm.

I was born on the farm. My dad was, I think, a real great person. So was my mother, although I didn't know her too well because she died when I was four. Both of them were able to accept this youngest child as one of the family and to give me the love and security all children need and which, certainly, all handicapped children especially require. I had four brothers and a sister; I never had any doubt that I was an accepted member of the family and just as good as anyone else. . .or probably even a little more important, according to my dad.

We lived on the farm for about four years; then we moved into town and opened up a greenhouse. When I was twelve we moved again, to St. Paul. My father became a gardener at Gillette Hospital, which specialized in work with handicapped children and where I'd been a patient myself.

That was kind of a hard move because I had to leave behind the kids I had grown up with in Grantsburg, who knew me in the neighborhood, and start all over again in a new place.

Youngsters are really very good about accepting disabilities. A lot of people say they are so cruel; they can be, because they can be very frank. But on the other hand, I think that they can accept differences much more easily than adults do. They just take you as you are.

That's what the kids in the old neighborhood did, so I had friends there. I grew up playing baseball and pum-pum-pullaway and all of those games, even though I couldn't run. They dragged me around in the wintertime on a sled, and when they roller-skated, they took me along in a wagon. So I grew up with a happy childhood.

What was it like, living in a society fifty years ago that really was not prepared to accommodate handicapped people? I'm thinking about current laws requiring handicapped parking spots, for example, and providing access to public buildings.

It is true that there has been a great change in the last — well, really just in the past ten or fifteen years as far as making accommodations easier for the handicapped.

Certainly one thing that society can do is have parking places for them, and have entrances into public buildings that are accessible. These things make it possible for them to be a part of society; otherwise it's so difficult to get places.

Even our churches have been offenders, you know. They used to build them up so high. The same is true of most older public schools, too. They are all going to have to change now.

The younger handicapped people feel that hardly anything is being done. But those of us who have been with it for awhile realize tremendous strides have been made.

When I went to the University of Minnesota, which was in 1934, they were happy to have me and were very pleasant and friendly and so on, but there were no elevators. If you could get there, that's fine. If you couldn't get there, it was too bad — you just didn't go.

You had a counselor at the University of Minnesota who told you to forget the idea of becoming a teacher, did you not? He didn't think it was in the cards for you. That must have been a discouraging moment in your life.

Yes. I had always thought that teaching was one thing I could do because I could talk. I didn't think you had to be too physically active to be a teacher. . .at least, some I had had weren't too active!

But it was the 1930s and the Great Depression, and there were a lot of teachers unemployed, and I suppose it was practical advice. . ."if you think you're going to get a job, think again because you just won't."

But it turned out that that's where I did get a job.

You also wanted to be a librarian and were discouraged from going into library science.

That's right. They wouldn't even let me take the course because they said that I couldn't do all that was required. The counselor whom I had, who headed the University Counseling Service, became a good friend of mine and tried to help me find a job. When I was considering library work, they told him, "What can she do? She can't stack books."

My friend said, "She's not going to be doing that when she gets through." But it didn't make any difference; they said you have to be able to carry and stack books, so I couldn't get into that.

And social work — I wanted to try that, too. But at that time the social workers pretty much went into the homes. The counselor said, "Well, you can't drive a car" — because at that time I couldn't, though I can now — so that was out too. It was kind of hard to know what I was supposed to do.

Didn't you write to a publishing company looking for work as a writer?

I wrote looking for work first as a proofreader, which is about as lowly a job as you can get, you know. I had my degree then, but I was willing to take that up just to get a job, thinking that maybe I could proceed up the ladder to editing.

But then the management of this particular publishing company, a large one in St. Paul, said they couldn't take me because of their insurance rates — you know, that I couldn't escape fast enough in case of a fire. I said I would be willing to take a chance, but they wouldn't hire me.

At that very crucial point in your life, didn't a minister friend get you back on your original track?

That's right. He was Dr. W.F. Schmidt, who had been president of the college that I attended for my first two years, Luther Academy. At that time he had become head of the religion department at Concordia College because ours had merged with one in Iowa and the St. Paul campus had closed.

He knew the superintendent of a small struggling school for crippled children in Fargo, the Good Samaritan School, and he told him about me. This was in August. Of course they couldn't pay very much, but they needed a teacher. They said that, if I came up for an interview, they might be interested. I did, and I got the job.

You weren't even qualified to teach at that time, were you?

No, and they didn't know it. The man who hired me, Mr. W.B. Schoenbohm, who now heads Courage Center in Minneapolis, was a minister and didn't know about education requirements. He just knew I had a degree, and I wouldn't say anything to bring my lack of education credits to his notice. I figured there were a lot of North Dakota teachers that weren't qualified, and I was right.

So you kept right on working toward your degree while you were teaching.

I had my bachelor of arts degree, but I did have to get those fifteen credits in education. Concordia was real good about it. They let me take a couple of courses over there while I was teaching in Fargo, and they let me take them as independent study. They also gave me credit for practice teaching. Then I went to the University of Minnesota that summer and picked up the rest of them, so I got myself qualified after I'd already been teaching.

You completed eight years of schooling in four years as a child — is that correct?

Well, that's right. That was in the elementary grades.

I was eight, you see, when I started school because they weren't used to handicapped kids in the public schools at that time. I don't know what they'd thought I was going to do as far as getting an education.

When I was eight, my dad went over to the principal and asked if I could enter school. He said, "Well, let's try her from Easter to the end of school."

So that's what we did, and it worked out fine. The principal got real interested after that. He was the one who kept double-promoting me.

In 1941 the Crippled Children's School came into your life. What was your first job there, Dr. Anne.

As a teacher. You see, I taught at the Good Samaritan School for Crippled Children in Fargo until it closed. It reopened in Jamestown in 1941 with a new building and under new management. We had been operated by the Good Samaritan Society, which went under the Lutheran Hospital and Home Society.

I taught junior high at Gillette Hospital in St. Paul for a year, just as a fill-in, between the times we closed up in Fargo and began again in Jamestown. Then I went into the new school at Jamestown as a high school teacher.

I taught anything and everything — even math, and I could hardly keep my own checkbook straight.

Did you ever consider that you might spend thirty-nine years at that school?

No — and I never dreamed I would become an administrator, either.

That was my next question. That happened in 1950. It must have been a big decision for the school's leadership, hiring a severely handicapped person — and a woman — to head their school, even though they knew you and your work after nine years of teaching.

Well, I think they did pretty much know who I was. And they were in a spot; it was July and they didn't have an administrator. That helped!

I had accepted a position in California that summer and was going to leave in August. Maybe you just become more valuable once you are going to leave. Anyway, they offered me the job.

I think it was quite unusual, too, both being a woman and being handicapped. Of course, being a woman isn't so different in education because you do have a lot of women administrators.

Tell us about the Anne Carlsen School today. How much has it grown over the years?

We have eighty-eight students right now, and all but six live on the campus. We have dormitories for them, two new dorms in which they live four to a room with a bathroom between two rooms. In the center is a lounge. Boys live on one side and girls on the other, so in the center they can be together. It's quite comfortable and it's attractive.

Everything is connected at the school. It's all on one floor, so it is spread out a lot. I would say it's a good two-block walk all the way around.

That's an advantage in some ways because the kids who are using crutches have to walk in order to get anywhere. That's one of our purposes — to help them become independent and, if possible, to walk. Many of them can't, but they have learned to live with wheelchairs as well as they can.

You must have seen some big innovations there in thirty years. You have certainly not gone without national recognition for the work you have been doing. What are some things of which you are proudest?

Well, of course we have grown a lot. We started with just one L-shaped building. Since then we have had seven building projects, each one unlike all the others.

Our student body has changed. When I first came to the school, I had almost entirely kids with polio. Now we just have one, and that one student comes from a foreign country.

Our youngsters are more severely handicapped today, so we also have a stronger rehabilitation program. When we opened in Jamestown we just had three teachers and one physical therapist, and she left after a couple of months. Now we have quite a staff of therapists. We have three physical therapists, two occupational therapists, and two speech therapists, all under medial direction. We have a medical staff in Jamestown and also some consultants from Fargo.

We try to have a coordinated program because rehabilitation is really a part of the education of the child. He needs to learn how to do things for himself, how to be independent in feeding and dressing and, if possible, in walking. So this is part of his educational program. It's scheduled just as classes are.

The students also have to learn all the things that other kids do. We feel that it is important that they get a basic education so that if they have the ability to go on to college, they can do it. If not, at least they can compete with others.

It may not be fair, but I think that the handicapped probably have to be better than non-handicapped in order to succeed.

That brings up the topic of mainstreaming. How do you feel about mainstreaming, the education of handicapped children in the same classrooms as those who don't have handicaps?

I don't believe it should be mandatory for every child, but it should be adopted for the youngster who can keep up with the rest of the stream.

I think mainstreaming can turn out in three ways, depending on the child. I think of it sometimes in terms of the youngster sitting on the bank and watching things go by. This is sometimes true. The child is simply in the classroom. He is allowed to listen and to be there, but he doesn't actually get to be part of the group and he doesn't do the work that he might be able to do if he had more individual help.

Then there's the youngster who is so far behind, who is just struggling so hard and yet can never catch up.

Finally, there's the youngster who may not be up with the top bunch, but he's right in there. I think that's the group which should be mainstreamed.

Of course, it's going to be much easier now with schools being built so that you don't have the bathroom down in the basement and you can get into the building easily. This is good because, after all, the handicapped are part of the society. They shouldn't be segregated.

But I think this has to be decided on an individual basis. The child who needs a lot of therapy and a lot of individual help would be better off in a special school for a time. We work to get our kids back to public school when we feel they are ready to compete.

The handicapped as a group seem better organized in the last five or ten years than any time in history. What's led to that organization? It's been so successful that theirs has become a rather loud voice in policy-making.

Yes, they have. They've actually become quite militant. especially the younger ones.

I think that they are beginning to recognize that they do have rights. In that sense they are taking a tip from the black civil rights movement and the women's movement, and feel that if they organize and make demands they can achieve something. And of course, they do have some leaders who are very capable.

I was in Washington a few years ago when they organized a march on the Capitol. They had the help of a lot of non-handicapped people, too, because many of them were in wheelchairs and it's a long way from the Washington Hilton down there.

And they have achieved some things, too, by making their demands.

What is the next step?

Transportation is one big issue. In many of the large cities all buses are being made accessible to the handicapped. I think Fargo has gone with having door-to-door transportation which, in many ways, seems to me more sensible for the severely handicapped; it's kind of hard for them to get to a bus stop and so on.

The White House Conference on the Handicapped created a number of recommendations on this subject and others that they're now trying to get through.

Education is one of the biggest things. We assume that all handicapped children are getting their education today because the law now says they should be. Yet about one-fourth of the physically handicapped in this country are not being educated today. And that's a lot.

However, as I mention when I give my talks, in 1940 it was some three-fourths. So, you see, it really has improved.

I think we are going to be hit a little bit by the economic crunch. But there is an awareness now of what the handicapped need, and it's going to go forward.

Looking down your resume, I see so many awards that I don't have time to read them all — the Golden Plate Award in 1975, National Teachers Hall of Fame in 1975, Theodore Roosevelt Rough Rider Award in 1966, Jamestown's Outstanding Citizen of the Year in 1967, Minnesota Outstanding Achievements Award in 1964, the President's Trophy for Handicapped American of the Year in 1948, and on and on.

How do you feel about awards like these, Dr. Anne — all these many plaques, plates, citations and dinners in your honor?

Well, they are kind of nice, I must say!

I think the President's Trophy was the beginning of those awards. You get one and it leads to another.

Recieving that one was rather special. I had hoped that President Eisenhower would be there to present it, but he was busy with Churchill. . .

You played second fiddle to Winston Churchill?

Yes, and so Vice President Nixon presented it to me instead. He was very nice. He told me he thought I should go into politics. He said he thought I would do well.

I don't quite see, though, why I should have gotten so many awards because I really haven't done anything too outstanding. The only thing I have done is buck the physical disability. We say that the handicapped can do anything if we just put them in the right place and so on. But when we do, they make quite a fuss over it.

I suppose I shouldn't really object to that, though. I do feel admiration myself for some who do well.

It seems that the non-handicapped world goes from one extreme to the other — first making it difficult, as a handicapped person, for you to get an education and find a job, and then almost trying to make you bigger than life when you succeed in spite of that.

That's true. You are putting it exactly right. It's almost embarrassing, you know. If I had written a book or poetry or a symphony or something more difficult, perhaps I could understand. But I really haven't done anything that outstanding, I don't think.

So you have to work on keeping your perspective — is that right?

I don't think I have too much trouble that way because I try to kind of laugh about it.

If I asked you, "Who is Dr. Anne Carlsen," how would you answer me?

That's a good question...well, I would say I'm a handicapped person who is just like most other people, who enjoys many of the same things and who has had the advantage of a job that's turned out to be a pretty good one.

It's had a lot of fringe benefits, too, such as the recognition. I got a trip to Australia on that basis, a six-week all-expenses-paid trip — you can't do much better than that!

Anne Carlsen is somebody who enjoys life and hopes to keep going for a few more years.

That brings up another topic. You had tendered your resignation at Jamestown recently and they talked you out of it, so to speak. You are going to be working for them for at least a while longer, I think.

Another year.

Good. May I ask what changed your mind, why you decided to stick around another year?

They were fairly convincing that they weren't quite ready yet to name a successor. And the closer that retirement got, the worse it looked to me. I wasn't sure I wanted every day to be a Saturday or a Sunday, so it wasn't too hard for them to change my mind — although, when I handed in my resignation, I really meant it. I was looking forward to some leisure time, and still am.

You know, when you've worked for forty-two years, that's quite a habit. It's a long time. In the service, you know, I could have been retired for twenty-two years now.

We all have trouble knowing what to say and do around handicapped people sometimes. I suspect newly handicapped people also have trouble around us...I say "us," meaning normal people, whatever that means. What can I do and what can you as a handicapped person do to make it easier to interact when we are together?

I think you probably are a natural at this, Boyd. Anyone who is considerate and thoughtful is going to do the right thing.

You offer help, and then you go along with what the handicapped person suggests. I think that's the thing: if you treat handicapped people as you would anyone else, with consideration, you can't go too far wrong. You should let them kind of set the tone, I think, and let them suggest how you can help, because it's pretty hard to know what's the right thing to do sometimes.

I think the handicapped person should recognize that sometimes the other person needs a few cues. You should be willing to say, "Do it this way" if you need help, or "oh, I can do it myself" if you don't need assistance. If handicapped people say they don't need help, it's probably better to let them go ahead and do it themselves.

I am not one of those real independent people. I am perfectly willing to let someone open the door for me, to help me in and so on. But if I can make it myself, I don't particularly care to be carried, because that's hard on the other person. If I can make it on my own, why, I am fairly independent.

Some people might think that working as you do with handicapped youngsters, some severely so, could at times be a most heartbreaking endeavor, and I am sure you have days when you question it too. How do you handle the discouragement that must sometimes be inevitable?

I think that's true. Dark days like that are bound to happen. But on the other hand, there are many times when you see achievement, too.

You must recognize that with youngsters who are severely handicapped, while the future isn't really going to be too bright, the training that they are getting is going to help make life a little richer and more satisfying for them.

Though you don't want to let yourself become hard, you have to be somewhat objective about that. Otherwise you wouldn't be able to do anything.

When you are around those kids, you know, you realize that they are just kids after all. They are like other youngsters; they are not weeping about their troubles, and that helps.

It's hardest when they hit their teens and twenties because you are more aware of what the demands are going to be. We see this period because we do have youngsters through high school. I am sure that a lot of them, when they become seniors, are happy because they are like any other kids: they are glad to have it done. And yet they have some doubts about what the future is going to be.

The school is a very secure surrounding for them right where they are.

Yes, yes, it is.

Do they frequently discover limitations sometime after they leave?

It's a protective environment, and this is a criticism, of course, from the outside world.

But on the other hand, maybe you need that for awhile in order to build up your self-confidence. These youngsters have a chance to participate. They can be president of the student council. They had a prom the other night and, earlier, a disco dance, and they were all dancing. Some of us said to each other, "Gee, they look normal."

Disco dancing — now, that's all right!

Louis L'Amour

Harold Schafer

U.S. Senator Quentin Burdick

U.S. Senator Milton Young

Roger Maris

Jim Adelson

Mike Morley

Bobby Vee (left)

Lawrence Welk (right)

Fritz Scholder

Agnes Geelan

Lenus Carlson

Ida Prokop Lee

Anne Carlsen *Cliff "Fido" Purpur*

Bobby Vee

I first saw Bobby Vee on stage in 1983. He was playing a Fargo club date to a packed house of fans who had come to hear him sing some of the songs that made him one of America's top male vocalists in the 1960s.

The audience loved him. They applauded wildly as the guy with the still-boyish good looks took them back in memory to a far less complicated time. . .to a time when their real major concerns were what to wear to Saturday's sock hop and whether that blonde from the North Side already had a date.

And as Vee moved from a noisy rock number to a romantic ballad, there were the smiling exchanged glances that said, "He's singing our song!"

Vee seems to have well survived the hectic years that saw him leave high school at sixteen to perform across the country to screaming, adoring fans. In a business where the pressures and schedules claim a lot of victims and where drugs and alcohol are an all-too-inviting panacea, the Fargo native has been able to keep sight of what he calls the most important thing — how we all feel about ourselves day by day.

Some of you know this young man as Robert Thomas Velline, but virtually everyone recognizes him by another name — Bobby Vee, the Fargo boy who rose to the top of the musical charts more than twenty years ago with "Susie Baby."

After years of living on the West Coast and traveling coast to coast, you've returned to make your home in the Midwest, in St. Cloud. Why, Bob?

Well, mentally I'd moved away from Los Angeles a couple years ago. I was wanting to get out of the big city and the smog and the congestion.

I don't know. . .I have never really gotten the Midwest out of my system, I guess. We have a lake cabin in Detroit Lakes, and we have brought the family back here every July and August. That has really been nice.

Let's go back to 1959. "Susie Baby" was the song. You were sixteen years old, and suddenly you were thrust into the limelight with your hit song. It brought national recognition — enormous prominence.

How does a sixteen-year-old handle it? Was it a difficult time for you?

Well, no — it wasn't really difficult. Basically it was fun!

I think the biggest decision that I faced in my life at that time was whether or not I should finish school. I had just completed my sophomore year at Fargo Central High School.

And the record came out — I think it was about in June when we began driving around the area to promote it. It was really only released at first up in this part of the country; I sold the records out of Minneapolis.

It cost us $500 to go into a studio to make the record. They gave us — oh, I don't know how many copies of the record as part of the deal. We went to work to promote it in the area. The radio stations started playing it, too. We were a local band and everybody seemed to be on our side.

So they played the record and, lo and behold, customers began creating a demand for it in the record stores. It really took off, and it was a nice progression.

We had been just looking for a way to broaden our horizons a little from a working standpoint, so that we could go out and get bookings for the weekends.

Then the record took off and went to Number One. Suddenly I had to decide to whether or not go back to school, whether to pursue music full-time.

What did you do?

I made an appointment with my school counselor back in Fargo Central High. He asked me, "Well, Bob, if everything fizzles out, will you come back?"

I had never really figured on that as an alternative, but I thought about it for a minute and then told him, "Yes." He set me up at the campus right here, North Dakota State University, for correspondence courses. And I studied that way and went out on the road to sing "Susie Baby."

One of your big breaks grew out of one of the most tragic moments in rock history. Of course, that was the plane crash that killed Buddy Holly when he was on his way from Iowa to a concert in the Moorhead Armory.

Sometime in the middle of the night before the concert was scheduled, there came a panic phone call to Bobby Vee to fill in for Buddy Holly.

Buddy, Richie Valens and the Big Bopper had chartered an airplane to fly from a concert in Iowa to Fargo-Moorhead. It iced up and crashed shortly after takeoff.

The show in Moorhead was already sold out by the time news reached here. Some of the performers had made it on time; they were traveling by bus instead of flying. The local promoters didn't want to cancel the concert. It was that old tradition, "the show must go on."

They were looking for a local band as filler, really, when they asked for advice from Charlie Boone, who was a disc jockey at KFGO at that time. He mentioned it on the air.

Excuse me — had "Susie Baby" been released yet?

No, "Susie Baby" wasn't out yet.

We were really just a church basement band — that kind of thing. One of the guys called Charlie at the radio station and said, "You know, we would like to fill in." The promoters told us to come on down.

We ran around in a panic trying to buy uniforms. We ended up at J.C. Penney's, buying some angora neckties for twenty-five cents apiece. I will never forget those ties. . .never did get the knot out of mine. I had to pull it off over my head at the end of the night.

We didn't even have a name for our band, and had to think one up on the spot.

So the Shadows came to be?

Right. The master of ceremonies asked, "What's the name of your band?" We just kind of looked at each other, and I blurted out, "The Shadows."

He went on stage and introduced us: "Here they are, the Shadows!" We walked out and stood there, just scared to death.

We had a limited repertoire. I think we probably did every song we knew — that would be six or seven.

Good reception?

The reception was very nice.

Buddy Holly had worked with a group called the Crickets for several years. They had split up just weeks before that plane crash, and there had been speculation at the time that they were going to get back together again.

You filled the void, in a way, after his death, doing some work with the Crickets yourself. Now, were they trying to make another Buddy Holly out of Bobby Vee at that time?

Oh, I never saw it that way, though I was a big fan of Buddy Holly and the Crickets.

"Susie Baby" was doing well in this area. We eventually sold the master to Liberty Records in Los Angeles, and they released it nationally. The guy who was responsible — the one who liked the record and bought it for Liberty — was a producer named Snuff Garrett, who had also been a good friend of Holly's.

When he heard our record, he thought it was reminiscent of Buddy Holly and the Crickets. So when I went out to Los Angeles to start recording, he arranged for me to use them on my recording sessions.

We had been looking for a concept for an album. It just seemed like a natural thing to do. The album was called "Bobby Vee Meets the Crickets." It went on to be the number one album in England.

It was really fun for me because, as I said, I was a big fan of theirs. It gave me a chance to do some good old rock and roll, too, of the kind I had grown up with here in the Fargo-Moorhead area.

You mentioned that the record album became a big hit in England. I am assuming that led to your concert appearances there in 1960.

Yes, we did the first concert tour over there and found really wonderful audiences. They really loved the American pop singers and American music, all kinds of music — dixieland, country, blues, rock and roll. They saw all that music as having originated in the United States, so they gave you some extra points for that.

When did you run into the Beatles? I believe you said you did a television show over there with them in 1962?

Yes, that was in either '62 or '63.

The Beatles, before they made it big worldwide a few years later, were just a regional band that was really hot in Liverpool. I'd been touring the country at the same time they were catching on.

In fact, I remember that while I was working in Liverpool, a reporter who was interviewing me said, "If you aren't doing anything after the concert, you should come down to the Cavern. There's a great band down there called the Beatles." He wrote for a publication called "Mersey Beat," which I thought at the time was some kind of religious publication.

Anyway, I never did make it down there on that trip to hear them. But by the time of the next tour the Beatles were really hot and they had a couple of records out. I did a British TV show with them that time.

You said the show was rather unusual — in what regard?

Television in England at that time was all government-controlled, so there was very limited choice of TV programs. If you were lucky enough to have a hit record that got you on TV, everybody saw you.

It was unusual for me in that the English musical phenomenon was just happening there, and I saw it begin. We had to push through five thousand people to get into the theatre. People were just everywhere — screaming kids, teenieboppers — waiting for the Beatles.

We did the TV show and it was really very nice. But to have seen another group happening on that large a scale was just kind of mind-boggling.

They hadn't even been discovered in the United States yet.

No, but they were already becoming very big in England.

When you heard the Beatles, did you think, "Hey, this group is going somewhere"? Was it that obvious?

It was obvious to me and, as a matter of fact, to my producer, who was there with me. Their product was only being released in England at the time, and he tried to buy the rights to release it in the United States.

They had had a couple of hit records by that time. They wanted $50,000 to sign a contract in the United States. . . which was really a tremendous amount of money at that time, though it's just a drop in the bucket in retrospect.

At the time, though, it was unbelievable. Elvis Presley had signed with RCA for $35,000, and here were four English guys who wanted $50,000. The record company just couldn't see their way through it. So they passed on that.

You had some great moments on "American Bandstand." In fact you and Dick Clark, its originator, are still pretty good friends. What was the atmosphere like on "Bandstand"? It always looked so very cool and relaxed. Was it that way on the set?

Yes, it really was. But it could mean a difference of a hundred fifty thousand to two hundred thousand copies in record sales. Dick's audience was huge, and it included all the record-buying public of the time.

But it was a relaxed, everyday kind of thing. He was used to it; he did a show with a different guest act every day of the week.

I used to arrive about ten minutes before it went on the air. Dick would point and say, "Just stand right here, and when you get to the bridge walk down over there, and then come back to me and we'll chat a few minutes afterwards." That was as elaborate and blocked out as it got.

You lip-synched the music, as I recall.

Right. I never really enjoyed the lip synchs, and it really does get to be difficult after awhile. It is hard to remember just exactly how you did the song and imitate it perfectly time after time after time, getting your mouth moving just the same way.

You mentioned the fact that you would go on that program and probably sell two hundred thousand more records. Dick Clark obviously was a very, very powerful man in the record industry. Did you get paid for your appearances on his program?

Yes, we got union scale. . .something like $130.

And that means that, although it was a national show, it still was a low-budget program. And then, of course, if you did a live performance it created a more expensive union situation, and it became prohibitively costly. That's why "Bandstand" only used lip synchs, isn't it?

Sure.

You were telling me earlier, Bobby, about touring in Italy and singing your hit songs in Italian — which you don't speak. How did you manage that?

Not very well, you can be sure, by a Norwegian boy from Fargo! I could just hear them thinking, "Oh, you're not fooling us, Velline."

They all thought at first that I was Italian — the name, you know.

It was crazy. "Run to Him" was a hit while I was touring there, and someone came up with the bright idea of doing it in Italian. They figured that would really establish me there. First I recorded the song in Italian — phonetically, because I don't know a bit of the language. Then the promoter let me know they'd lined up an appearance on a national TV show, too.

I was panicking. I thought, "My God, I don't even know what the words mean."

I had cue cards, and they were huge — each was the size of a big door. I wrote it all out, phonetically you know, and the Italian crew couldn't even tell what it said because I spelled it so I could pronounce it.

I tell you, my eyes were glued to that card! If I had lost my place just once, I would have never known when to come back in again.

I went on to record two or three songs in Italian, though.

How did it go?

You know, I don't really know. I don't think that people were really so interested in hearing things in their native tongues instead of English as we thought they were.

I was in South America again earlier this year and did a television show, and noticed that people were singing along with "The Night Has a Thousand Eyes" and whatever else I did, even though they didn't speak English. I found it kind of amazing.

Earlier you mentioned all the screaming fans you encountered in England, and we've often seen news films or movies depicting fans trying to reach their favorite stars. You had that experience too, I've read, with fans ripping off your coat or part of your clothing as you left a concert in Ohio. What happened that day?

It was so out of control there. I had almost expected things like that to happen in England, where the scene was already so big, but not here.

It had been a surprise there, too, at first. They used to close concerts with "God Save the Queen" on my early tours; people would just be rocking along and suddenly they'd all just stand up, as still as can be, and we could exit and get to the bus for our getaway.

But in the United States the really frantic years had been in the 1950s. I was a pop singer in the early '60s and not expecting that from Americans anymore.

What you're talking about happened just as I walked offstage after doing a Dick Clark show in Toledo. A girl came running up behind me, screaming, and grabbed the back of my jacket. She split it right up the back, all the way to the neck.

As I said, it seemed out of context. People hadn't been acting that way. I couldn't believe it. I just looked at her funny and said, "You ripped my jacket!"

Were you frightened?

It confused me. I sure wasn't used to that kind of reaction.

When the crowds started stomping and whistling and running in the aisles, were you ever frightened for your personal safety at a concert?

Oh, a few times I have been.

I used to do concerts sponsored by radio staions, who'd call them appreciation shows. They brought in national acts and then opened them up for their listeners.

I did one at Lake Pontchartrain near New Orleans that must have drawn a hundred thousand people. It was huge. As people got caught up in the rhythm of the music and swayed back and forth, I could feel the stage — it was really makeshift — moving under me.

You just say a prayer in a case like that and keep on singing "Susie Baby."

Have you worked with many of the great stars you'd admired yourself while you were growing up here in the 1950s?

I have met a lot of them and worked with a lot of them.

Growing up in the '50s, I was a big Elivs Presley fan. In the mid-70's my wife and I went to Las Vegas to see him perform, along with a Los Angeles disc jockey friend and Dick Clark and his wife. I didn't know it at the time, but not even Dick had met him.

There were several celebrities in the audience and Elvis introduced various people. When he got to Dick Clark, the place just went crazy.

Elvis is so big a star, but he is such a nice man. We were invited backstage afterwards. That was right before he started going out to do his tours across the country and I remember him asking all kinds of questions about what it was going to be like in Des Moines. I jumped in and said, "Oh, I know all about Iowa and the Midwest."

He was very nice, and he just had an amazing charisma about him.

Another memory of the 1950s is payola. I was working in radio at KNOX in Grand Forks, making $1.25 an hour working on weekends. We had never heard of payola — we got left out somehow!

But to refresh the memory of people who might not remember that era: disc jockeys were getting money from record companies or even from recording stars, in some cases, for playing their records. What was your vantage point during the payola scandals, Bobby?

I think that was more prevalent in the 1950s. But I must admit that I was very young when I started out and I was probably pretty naive. I didn't see that part of it. I am sure that some of it went on. It was just nice gifts or sweaters or a weekend in Las Vegas. . .that kind of thing. I think a lot of that stuff was kind of hard to track.

I was aware of it happening in the blues field. Generally, what would happen when a disc jockey was on the take was that he would get $50 from this distributor and $50 from that distributor, and — you know — end up with a few hundred bucks in his pocket at the end of the week to play their products. Of course the Federal Communications Commission came down on that.

Dick Clark at that time had some problems. He owned some publishing companies, and they said that he was showing favoritism in the songs that he played on "American Bandstand" because he owned the product.

There was another rumor — let's see if we can clear this up once and for all — that even though they were paid union scale or whatever, the artists who appeared on "American Bandstand" were expected to turn their checks back to Dick Clark. I heard the story more than once while I was a disc jockey myself. Is there any truth to that?

Never, as far as I was concerned. I always got my $130 bucks, smiled, said, "Thanks, Dick," went to Penney's and blew the money on a new angora tie to bring back to Fargo!

How about your management in those days? Now, you were sixteen years old. Obviously you had to have somebody managing your affairs and the money that you were making. Was it kept in trust? How did you handle that? It all happened very fast.

Yes, it did.

The fellow who was managing us at the start was from Fargo. His name was Bing Bingston and he ran the Moonlight and the Starlight Drive-In Theatres — he was our show business contact. He booked us around the area.

After "Susie Baby" came out he kind of lost interest. I don't know if he didn't think we were going to go any further or what. So I signed with a manager in Los Angeles.

I was so lucky when I got into this business. I was involved with a lot of good people. You hear stories about people being cheated on their royalties by their record companies...well, I always got my money. Oh, they may have beaten me out of a little, but that's a tough thing to keep tabs on.

We had a trust fund set up through the court system here in Fargo. California, of course, is really strict on minors because of child actors and all, Hollywood being the show business capital that it is. So when I turned twenty-one I received quite a chunk of money. I had been divvied out an allowance until twenty-one. I was thankful for that.

You mentioned the Hollywood atmosphere. What was it like from your vantage point out in Hollywood or in Los Angeles — was it as wild and crazy as we are led to believe?

I never liked Hollywood. I think it is a sleazy city.

I recorded in Hollywood and my record company's offices were in Hollywood, but I just avoided it at all costs.

That is obviously why you are back near home, in Minnesota.

Yes.

How about your traveling now? You were down in Santiago, Chile, a year ago doing a program there. What other kinds of things are you doing now?

In the last couple of years I have really been putting more focus on writing and publishing — getting into the behind-the-scenes part of the business.

I have been traveling for twenty-one years, and the road keeps getting longer.

And you are not quite forty yet — am I right?

I am thirty-eight.

How has your writing been going?

It's coming along.

I've always written as a hobby, ever since I was tiny. I guess it's really in the last few years that I've been getting more serious about it — deriving some pleasure from it, and really learning about it. I've been kind of honing it, I guess.

How about the musical trends — what is your reaction to the music we are listening to today? Obviously the disco beat is gone, for better or worse. What's your opinion of where popular music is going?

Well, I don't know. I don't think anybody ever really knows. And I am not sure disco is dead. I think disco has fulfilled a need for dance music. There is some tremendous talent out right now. But then, there always is great product out on the market. This seems to be the era for the cross-overs — music that blends both rock'n'roll and country or other musical trends.

I want to talk about trends. On an album cover from the early 1960s, there you are complete in the sweater, the Perry Como look (or the Bobby Vee look — whatever you prefer), short trimmed hair. . .super clean-cut all-American-looking. You had to be able to shift gears in the business as far as musical trends as well as dress and that sort of thing. When both the music and young people's style of dressing and appearance changed so drastically toward the end of the decade, how did you react?

I guess I had the fortune, or misfortune — however you want to look at it — of growing up on wax and vinyl. My, the changes I have gone through! My class pictures have sort of been recorded on my album covers, and I have gone through a lot of changes myself.

It began with five years of good fortune. Everything we released in our first five years was on the charts. And then music started changing — the English invasion, with the Beatles and Rolling Stones and all the other groups. I was getting air play during those years but not selling any records.

Yet in the late 1960s we came back with a song that became the biggest selling song of my career called "Come Back When You Grow Up."

At that point I really started evaluating what it all meant to me. I was out on the road working with big bands doing the hotel circuit, and just really not having fun. That re-evaluation prompted me to really start to get tough about the reasons that I had been attracted to music in the first place.

I went back to my roots — some of the country music I'd grown up with in the Fargo-Moorhead area, rock'n'roll and pop. The results are in the album from the early 1970s called "Nothing Like a Sunny Day." That's the one with the beard . . .that was another phase I went through.

As an artist, you had almost unparalleled success, with everything you did making the charts for five years. You rode terribly high for a long, long time.
Now, suddenly that popularity started to wane and the records didn't sell quite as much. What is that like for the artist? Does a certain terror and fear set in while you say, "My God, I am not as big as I was — what's happening?"

A little bit, yes — I went through that, especially in the mid-1960s when things were becoming so obviously different. San Francisco was happening with the flower children and folk rock, and everything really was changing.

I was looking for hit songs, songs that I thought would be hit songs. I'd go in and record a piece of material and think, "Well, this will be a hit." But it wouldn't. You experience a lot of frustration.

That is when I went through the period of looking at what it truly meant to be in the music business. I realized that, really, what was important was that I was doing things that I enjoyed.

I enjoy a low profile anyway. The idea of being Kenny Rogers really doesn't appeal to me. I enjoy music. I enjoy performing. I enjoy singing. I especially enjoy recording, incidentally, and I'm looking forward to more of that coming up.

But the important thing for all of us is, really, how we feel about ourselves on a day-to-day basis.

You mention that you would get a new song and say, "I hope this is a hit." Have you ever recorded other songs and instantly known that they were going to be as big as they finally became?

Yes, one of the gifts that you enjoy when you are sixteen years old is the ability, in your mind, at least, to conquer the world. I will tell you — when I was sixteen years old, it all just made sense to me. We went in and cut "Susie Baby," and I thought, "That is a good record. That sounds like a hit to me" — you know. I wasn't cocky or arrogant about it, but it just made sense. When things make sense, they make sense! That simple.

When the record came out and people started to play it, I just thought, "Well, sure. It's kind of a good record." It was only what I expected. I kind of like that confidence, looking back. And it became a hit.

How about later on? Any other songs you were sure about?

"Take Good Care of My Baby," which went to number one. I thought to myself, "It's a hit record," and it was.

And another one. . .well, it's like gambling, I suppose. You forget the many times when you thought, "This is a hit record," and nothing happened.

Have you ever recorded a piece of music that you wish you had not recorded — that you wish you could buy up all the copies and stick them in an attic somewhere?

That actually happened, quite a few times in fact, not actually buying them up but really wishing I could!

The way in which I was recording back in the 1960s was very different from what they're doing today. Music was recorded live. We'd actually do four songs in three hours. They'd crank up the band and rehearse them a couple of times — as a full orchestra — and then we'd run with it. I would come back, maybe, and do a double harmony part or something. There was none of the track-by-track recording and re-recording you see today.

There are a lot of clams in there. I hear them and I cringe a little bit.

What kind of songs are you singing now? Things you like?

I am mixing my shows up. I try to balance them between new material and the old hit songs that the people generally come to hear, and I do a little bit of country and a couple of bits from the 1950s including a Buddy Holly medley.

I mix them with things that I have either recorded recently and plan to release or new songs that I have written. So I get to stretch myself a little bit, too. Then it becomes a fun evening for me as well as the audience.

Have your fans changed since the early years of swooning teen-agers who requested pictures and wrote you long gushy letters?

Yes, the letters have changed a lot.

There was a gal in Fargo-Moorhead, a dear friend who kind of ran a fan club in this part of the country. She looked after all that stuff. If there was something that needed special attention, she would call me up or I would stop by and we would answer them. There was a lot of fan mail through the early 1970s. It is interesting to me that she has continued to correspond with a lot of those people throughout the years over the miles.

As I travel around today, people come up occasionally who were members of that old fan club. That's kind of fun, you know — that we can meet today as friends.

We have seen the tragic death of a number of musicians in the last half dozen years — Elvis, Mama Cass, Janis Joplin, Jimi Hendrix, and so many others, many of their deaths related to drugs. Is that a reflection of the tremendous pressures that entertainers are under? How do you deal with it?

Yes, I realy do believe that the tremendous pressure deserves part of the blame. You have to reserve some space for yourself and be able to detach yourself — leave your work at the office, so to speak — and equalize yourself.

Especially when you are really hot, there's always a dangerous possibility of believing your own hype and then trying to live up to those huge stars that we place over our celebrities' heads.

Well, you have come through some tumultuous times and don't look any the worse for wear. You look unscarred. At the ripe old age of almost thirty-eight, you seem happy and secure in what you are doing. Maybe you are going to write another hit one of these days. Do you ever think about that?

I have been writing more and more, as I said — spending more time on the publishing, and working with several other writers in the area here. There's a lot of talent in the Midwest, and we are providing at least one vehicle for national exposure. We're getting their tunes out to Nashville and Los Angeles.

I am excited about that because there is, and always has been, a lot of talent in this part of the country. The problem is only that people have just not known where to go.

Mike Morley

For the past thirteen years Mike Morley, a native of Minot, has been part of the predominantly faceless and nameless crew of professional golfers in the United States who follow the sun in search of a slice of the multi-million-dollar pie of prize money offered by the sponsors of Professional Golfers' Association tour events.

In that span of more than a dozen years Morley has won a single event, made a good run at the top spot on half a dozen occasions, and picked up over $400,000 in prize money.

Morley is no longer a regular on the main tour today. The main tour is reserved for the top money winners and exempt players who have been winners on the tour or who consistently finish in the top twenty. At the present time the state's most famous touring pro is playing on the second tour, a collection of falling and rising stars looking for a first or second chance at the big prize money.

Since our conversation, Mike has authored a book on putting, played a few tournaments in Asia, and examined some business opportunities unrelated to golf. He seemed then, and seems now, to be a young man at the crossroads. This is how he assessed his game two years ago: "I've had a lot of trouble being able to hit the ball in the last three years. If I can't improve on that, my career might be over."

Mike, you're certainly North Dakota's most famous touring pro today and probably its only one. In North Dakota golf history, I think only Paul O'Leary has ever really taken a crack on the pro tour. Am I right about that?

I think you are correct there. Paul played for quite a few years out there, though, and he is still competing.

Let me ask you a question prompted by a comment Celtic basketball star Bill Russell made 'way back in 1970. I was doing an interview with him and asked how he reacted to the naming of golfer Arnold Palmer as "athlete of the decade." They were contemporaries, of course. Russell kind of laughed that a golfer would get that honor; like many people, he didn't consider them athletes in the same sense as baseball or football players.

How do you, Mike, characterize a golf pro in terms of being an athlete?

Well, as far as the award they gave Arnold — they gave it to him because he did more for sports than anyone else did in that ten-year period. After Walter Hagen left, golf fell a long way for awhile. Arnold showed how it should be played, and the people identified with him and they loved him.

The only way I can really answer that question is that if you have ever seen Arnold Palmer live, I think you'll agree with me that he is the most impressive-looking athlete I have ever seen.

You know, golf is a combination of a sport, an art and a lot of things all together — not just pure physical contact at all. It's much more than that.

Let's talk about Mike Morley the athlete. I know you have taken some steps to improve your game. That would be similar to what a running back or a basketball player might do, isn't it?

I have felt one of the things that I have had trouble with over the years is that my body has not been able to handle the pace of ten months out in the heat. When you are in the heat a lot, you really can't eat much. You get so that your body really doesn't regenerate itself so well.

I started a weight-training program last fall. I lifted weights and worked out and ran.

Really, I don't know whether it has helped or not. I got off to the worst start this winter that I have had in quite a few years. But I feel better overall.

Golf is obviously a very physiological game. You would assume that once you have the swing all grooved and you know how to hit the shots, you should be able to shoot a sixty-eight any time you want. . .at least, the casual fan looks at it that way. But a great deal of it has to be mental.

Golf is almost all mental once you get to a certain level. You never have the same feeling that you had the day before.

That's what perhaps makes it a little harder than other sports. They play with a complete reflex and they can repeat the moves all the time. In golf, the physical feel is different every day. Some days you have it, and some days you don't.

But mentally, you can have it every day. You see some, like Nicklaus, who have it every day. You can get by when you are not playing real well physically and still shoot a low round. But if you are mentally not right, you will never shoot a low one.

Has inconsistency been one of the bugaboos for Mike Morley on the tour? You open with a sixty-nine, come back with a seventy, then maybe get a seventy-six, and your fans nod and say, "Gee, he always seems to have that one bad round."

Actually, at one time back about 1976 or 1977, I could play pretty well consistently. I used to get hot streaks. I was a streak player, and when I would get on a good roll, I would really go.

I haven't had a hot streak for three years, though, almost. In fact, I play just about the way I did right in between my hot streaks.

The reason I have been inconsistent is that I just haven't played very well every day. On three out of four days I am able to score OK, but I can't seem to keep it together for four straight days.

Where are you right now in your career development and where you might want to be — say, if you had a timetable. Where is Mike Morley's game right now at age thirty-four?

Well, my game is not where I want it to be right now. I can putt better, I chip better, I am better around the greens and I am, if anything, more competitive than I used to be.

My biggest drop, in fact, is that I have had a lot of trouble being able to hit the ball in the last three years. And that's what has really held me back. If I can't improve on that, my career might be over with.

I believe I can change it; this fall I am going to go about it again. I tried last fall some. I am going to go to a different teacher, a teacher I think can help me with what I need now.

What is that?

I need to incorporate more of a body turn back and through the shot. I have gotten too much of an arm swing. And that adds to my inconsistency.

Observers have said that Ben Hogan, late in his life, was still as good a player as you could find from tee to green. But it's said that, in the good golfers, when the game goes it's usually on the putting green. Is that safe to say?

Well, it happens to some people. It depends on your stroke and your concept for putting.

I don't think that's ever going to happen to me. I'm a much better putter than I ever was. When I was a real good player, probably my biggest drawback was that I wasn't that good of a putter. I am a much better putter now.

In fact, this year, if I hadn't putted well, I don't know where I would have been. I had my best putting year by far this year. My putting was consistent.

In fact, I saw somewhere that you rank right up there with the top putters in the tour.

That's because I missed all the greens! Here I was always chipping up and putting the short putt.

I'm a weekend golfer — a lot of your fans are. We sometimes will be over in a rough and, when no one is looking, we will take that club and kind of tee it up a little bit. . .maybe even when we aren't supposed to.

I wonder if the opportunity presents itself to players on the tour. You are on your honor out there. Are there opportunities for the pros on the tour to tee it up a bit — in blatant words, to cheat? Does it happen?

I'm not saying it doesn't happen or that it hasn't happened, because it has. But it's at a complete minimum and the good players all play by the rules. They have a lot of golf etiquette and they play by the rules, and that's the way it is.

But you know, when you are down at the bottom struggling, trying to get on top, there are a lot of things that motivate people. I am not saying it doesn't ever happen.

So, in other words, you are for the most part on your honor when you are roaming around out there.

We are. But we used to play twosomes some years ago; one of the reasons they changed it to threesomes was for that particular reason. One against one in an argument isn't any good, but two against one is a little different story.

Ever since that has happened, there really isn't any cheating that I can see.

How are you paired up in a tournament? Do they decide what threesome goes where? Do they draw for that?

It's a draw, but there are different categories. The first two days, you play with the same group at different times. If you play late one day, you play early the next, or if you play early the first day, you play late on the next. Everybody kind of gets an OK shot at everything weather-wise.

But they pair you by categories, several categories. In one of them they pair the rabbits together, and then they pair the consistent money-winners together, and they pair the tournament winners together.

I get paired with the tournament winners. So on Friday and Saturday, or Thursday and Friday, I could get paired with Jack or Trevino or any one of them, anybody who's won a tournament out of a draw.

Now, some of the golfers are there because they are top money winners, but how does that field fill out for your basic tournament?

Well, many players are exempt. There are a lot of ways to be exempt — they pick the top six money winners or, back before about 1963, if you won the PGA or the U.S. Open you were exempt for life.

They have some other categories for your career earnings that you get an exemption on. They take the rest of the guys who want to come in for the tournament. The remainder of the field is filled with Monday morning qualifying rounds.

It just depends on how many exempt players make the cut the week before; it also determines if you are in the tournament the next week. If you finish in the top twenty-five — say, just for instance, the Quad City Tournament — this year, you are exempt next year.

So there are several ways to get exempt. They fill the field up with exempt players and then all the non-exempt players get together and play Monday morning.

Where are you right now in your career, as far as being invited to play in tournaments? Are you in pretty good shape in that regard?

Well, no. . .I don't get invited to play in that many tournaments. I mean, they also have a category of eight sponsors' exemptions, and they give them to guys like Chichi — you know, guys who attract quite a crowd. They don't give too many of those to me. But I don't ask for them.

So you are still fighting yourself into that starting line of the industry.

That's right. But I have only had to qualify something like five times in the last three years, so it's really not anything serious.

I haven't missed a cut on a tour since the Houston Open back in April or May. I haven't had to qualify since then, so it hasn't been that much of a hassle.

Where does all the money the tournaments give away come from? Where do they get that $400,000 purse, with the winner taking sixty grand and so on down the line?

It comes from all different sources of sponsors and things. A tournament doesn't have any trouble financially at all in the right area. The Pro Am has probably fifty teams of four amateurs who put up anything from one to two thousand dollars for one day of play.

Just to play with a pro.

Just to play. So say it was a thousand dollars — that's $200,000 in revenue right there.

Television has been a lot of help. All the tournaments go into a television pool, whether each tournament is televised or not; they all get a share of the pool, so even tournaments that don't have television broadcasts get a chunk of the money.

And the gallery brings in a lot. Some tournaments draw one hundred eighty thousand people.

Sure. And they pay twenty or thirty dollars' admission a day?

They don't pay that much at most of them, like in Greensboro, where they might pay ten dollars. But at the major tournaments they'll pay twenty dollars.

Are these tournaments basically put together by sponsors for charitable causes, Mike?

Right — that's the way they do it. So whatever is left over is given to charity. The tournaments are mostly non-profit.

Who do you like to play with? Do you have some favorites?

Well, my all-time favorite to play with was Sam Snead. I just loved playing with him, but I haven't played with him for about three years now.

He was just a real treat to play golf with. By the time you get done playing with him, by about the fifth hole, you are swinging so well that you can't believe it. . .just by watching him.

He has had some putting problems, also, that we talked about earlier. Is he still doing that strange-looking putting?

There's nothing wrong with Sam Snead's putting! Sam complains about his putting, but there's nothing wrong with it. He putts well.

What kind of conversations do you have when you move around the course? We get the feeling, watching on television, that it's a pretty grim scene. Everybody is marching up there deep in concentration. Do you ever go back and forth and chat on the way around?

Sometimes.

What do you talk about?

Depends on the other person. You know, it depends on if you get paired with a good friend of yours or whatever. If a guy likes to talk, I will talk some, but generally there isn't much conversation.

How about side betting? Golf is a game for bets, you know. No matter where you go, the weekend golfers place a few bets on the outcome of their games. Does side betting take place in the tournaments?

There's more gambling among the rabbits, probably, than there is amongst the good players.

Describe the rabbits for the fans who aren't familiar with the term.

A rabbit is a non-exempt player — just a guy that's trying to make it on the tour, and probably having a tough time. He is playing a lot of Monday qualifiers and maybe missing a lot.

He's leaving the town where this week's tournament is being played on Monday night or Tuesday, going on to the next town the week before the tournament begins and practicing to try to get ready for his next qualifier. So he actually left town before the present tournament is even played.

But he is called a rabbit because he just gets a little nibble at the lettuce.

Yes.

Well, obviously, there's a lot of betting going on.

Well, a lot of those guys are gamblers. I wouldn't say there's a lot of betting, but there are some pretty good-sized games also. There used to be some fairly decent games, more than now, but I think that's been busted up.

Is there anything in the rules of the tour that prohibits that kind of thing?

They don't like it. I mean, they frown upon it. So there really isn't much of it, not like you even see out at the country clubs across the United States. There really isn't much gambling.

There's enough of a gamble for us every day with the tournaments going on. I have never seen any gambling going on during a tournament round. Maybe just once in awhile on a Monday or Tuesday.

Mike, you've won just one tournament in your career. I recall the time — was it at the Heritage? — when you and Trevino were going head-to-head, and you got the great bounce coming into one of the greens that left you perhaps a stroke away from winning.

I am sure you remember that day. You bounced it off a steel pipe sitting somewhere and came on the green. What's it like when you are in there that close and you say, "I have a chance to win one?" Can you describe what that pressure is like?

I have had a lot of chances to win many tournaments, and the reason I didn't win in most of those cases was myself. I had the destiny of several tournaments in my hand and couldn't get it to the last green.

The time you describe was just one of those things that happened. I had a lot of trouble winning the first time. I think the first time I had a chance to win I was in Jacksonville. I had a one-shot lead going in the last round, and I got paired with Arnold Palmer for the first time in the last round.

I hit the ball about ten feet on the first hole. Nobody clapped. Then he hit a diving hook with a six-iron over the back of the green, and the people went wild. I knew right there that it was going to be a long day!

As it turned out, Ziegler shot sixty-five and won the tournament, and I came in second.

Coming from North Dakota, there was some intimidation for me in meeting those guys and seeing them play. I never lived around a place where they had a tournament that meant I could see pro golfers like them every day so that watching them would have been old-hat for me. So I was actually intimidated.

The next time I had a good chance to win was at Pebble Beach. I got paired with Nicklaus the first time. The only thing that kept me from winning was my nerves. I missed four three-foot putts in the first eight holes, and I still got a one-shot lead.

But my putting stroke was gone. I was just nervous. I was intimidated. . .and then Jack shot forty-five on the last nine holes. The people were going crazy, and it was pretty hard to keep everything back in perspective.

Did your knees actually knock sometimes when you were lining up a putt?

They might have done that! Generally, no. But that day, a lot of excitement was going around, and it was tough. We weren't playing with another pro player. We were playing with our amateur partners. It was kind of hard. If there would have been another player in the group, it might have made it a little easier.

You mentioned being paired with Palmer or Nicklaus. So often on television, when you see a younger or less well-known pro paired with stars like them, the fans seem to stand around the green and wait only until Jack or Arnie has putted. Then they go storming to the next tee box, even while the other player is still putting. . .

Those guys are really good about that, though. They will mark a ball from six inches or three inches or whatever to hold the people there.

Often you will putt out, you know, if you have a two-footer or a two-and-a-half footer and you're not in anybody's line; I will do that. But they will hold off on that if you haven't putted yet, because you know what can happen — especially if they have, like, a fifteen-footer and they make it. Then the people take off running.

Are the fans basically pretty well behaved on the tour? The ones on television seem to be, but do you have any fans who seem to get under your skin?

Greensboro is notorious for that. They put out a real community-type tournament, and they are a bunch of good old boys down there. They used to let them carry their beer up-course. Now they make them buy a beer there, and it's about three times as expensive, so they don't get in as bad shape as they used to.

And they play a different golf course. They used to play a golf course down there where the sixteenth hole was about a two hundred-thirty yard par-three all surrounded by water downhill into the wind. They would sit around there and just have a good time — watch the guys make seven or eight and just laugh at them.

How much control does the Professional Golfers Association have over players in terms of appearance — hairstyle, for example, or what kind of clothes you wear on the tour? Do they dictate to you on that regard at all, Mike?

They make it be known what they want to see, which I think is right. The tour is like a show. You should look good.

There are quite a few young guys coming up who don't care about things like that, and it actually turns people off. For their own selves' good, you know, they should try to clean themselves up. The PGA doesn't like to see beards out there, and you can't wear Bermuda shorts or jeans. I don't see anyone wearing jeans.

So there are no rules written in the books somewhere. The word has just been passed.

We do have a dress code. Enforcing it is something else again. The guys have been pretty good about it, though.

Talking about the behavior on the course, we saw something extremely unusual on television that came to mind when you mentioned the PGA rules. Was it Trevino who offered the advice to Watson on a shot that was carried by his microphone to the fans at home? Tell us about that incident.

The guy who produces the programs for CBS was responsible in a way for that.

CBS does by far the best golf coverage of any network.

I have seen them do tournaments where they show every shot everybody hits coming in, so you can see the whole thing in your mind. They're great with golf. But the executive in charge had the idea that microphones would add to it, you see. He's been trying to get the players to wear them.

Well, there are only a couple guys that really should wear mikes — Trevino and maybe Fuzzy — because really, it's not that interesting. Gets pretty dull, in fact.

But so Trevino had a mike on his caddy, and apparently some viewer in California who is a real purist on the rules heard Watson giving him some advice, some sort of advice about his swing or something. I don't know; I didn't see it.

Some fellow called up and complained. It didn't make any difference in the outcome of the tournament, but Watson got a two-shot penalty.

Trevino said, "That's the end of the mike!" It was devastating for the idea of using mikes. It was the end of it for him, and if they can't mike Trevino, then it's not working very well.

You mentioned only a couple of guys were worth putting the mike on, maybe Fuzzy Zoeller and of course Trevino. That's one of the complaints on the pro tour — that golfers can be kind of colorless people who go about their duties very grimly. We used to see fun-loving fellows like Champagne Tony Lima, but not too many of them are left anymore.

Did you ever watch Champagne Tony play golf? He was never all that exciting to watch play. Those reputations are really whatever the press makes you out to be, and not necessarily the way you are in person.

I'll tell you what — there are a lot of guys with color out there. They don't necessarily show it on the golf course, though. It's pretty grim work.

But that's one of the complaints, that the game lacks color.

Let me put it to you another way. I don't believe that golf was ever intended to be pushed to the extreme as entertainment like they push it today, with television and all the fans and all.

I think it's way too hard mentally on the players. It's just done to produce a kind of product that the fans across the United States want to see.

And being a part of it — when you are trying to push it to that limit, I can say that it's very, very hard mentally on the people that play.

Golf is a more of a mental drain than probably any of the other sports. So many variables enter into it, and there are so many elements involved. The players out there are really not very happy.

When you say they aren't very happy...

Well, Trevino enjoys playing golf. It's fun to watch him golf. But I have seen the nicest guys in the world lose control of themselves out there.

The game was made to be enjoyed. People go out there and play to enjoy it — have fun, get outside, and have a good time. It was never meant to be pushed to the farthest ability that Man could push it.

Tony Jacklin, who won the U.S. Open and the British Open, said that the difference on a four-foot putt and the pressure involved in making it is whether you are early on in your life and the tour. If you're just starting, you have to be aware that only if you make that putt, do you have groceries and gas money for another week.

The pressures are removed a little bit when you've already made a million dollars and you have some bucks in the bank. Then if you miss that putt, you are still going to go on with the tour and be able to pay your expenses.

Is that a fair appraisal?

Yeah, I would say that's fair. But I would say you probably make more of them when you need it for grocery money. They are easier to stand over when you have some money in your pocket, but actually, you probably make more of them when you really have to.

When you started on the tour, you were backed by a group of sponsors in Minot — is that right, Mike?

Right.

How long did that agreement last?

The first time, they sponsored me for one year and there were twelve guys who had a part of it. The deal lasted for one year, and I gave them part of my earnings for the next five.

I went on my own the second year. During the third year I had a little trouble, and the fourth year, so they got together and helped me again. Some of them did; there were some different guys involved that time.

I have been on my own ever since.

Somebody mentioned to me, "Gee, Morley is having a great year. He has made over forty grand." But I would guess it takes about that to keep you going on the tour.

This is actually the worst year that I have had in the last six years, as far as the earnings. I have played in a couple small tournaments and done OK, so financially I am not having a bad year. . .but just playing-wise on the tour, it's been hard.

What would it cost for a young pro today, going out and trying the big tour? What kind of budget would he have to have to get by with decent meals and stay in some decent motels and, say, try it for twelve months?

It's hard to answer that question because it varies.

The better you play, the more it costs you. You pay your caddy a percentage, five or six percent. That could make a difference for you of two or three hundred bucks a week.

When I first went on the tour, I think I got $13,300. I would say that I could not get by with any less than three times that. We are talking $40,000, but I have played out there long enough that I am not going to stay in a dumpy motel, eat bad food or whatever. If I can't make it out there without having to skimp and skimp and skimp every day. . .

When your playing days are over — that might be two years, ten years, who knows — a lot of pros move into a club somewhere and become a club pro. Do you look to that in the future, or to something else, maybe?

Well, I hope I don't have to do that. But I am not saying I wouldn't. I would probably enjoy it. But really, as far as my outlook is right now, I would say I would try to get into something else.

We will just have to see

You said it should be fun out there on the golf course. From where you are right now, is the game still fun for Mike Morley? Do you still find yourself looking forward to those tournament weekends?

Golf is fun when you are playing well.

It still is fun when I am playing well, but it's not fun when I'm not. I have done it for so long! It's just about the only thing that I have done for the last twenty years, and, just like anything else, it gets old after awhile.

The thing I don't like about it most — not saying that I don't like it — is playing it all back in my mind and trying to make it right. All the time! Every day!

I can't take a day off. Other people can go to the lake or whatever and get away from their work. I can't shut my mind off and forget about golf because if I am working on something, say my swing or whatever, most of the practicing is done in my head without even hitting balls.

It's too tough during the year to cut that off. You can't even take a day off; you can't lay it all down for a week and say "That's it." By the time I go back to Arizona at the end of the tour, it will take me three weeks to wind down. I will just be hyper for weeks at the end of the year.

It's that pressure, the mental process of golf, again.

Even the casual North Dakota golf fan always looks down the list to see if Morley is there in the opening or the second round. We're all wishing you the best of luck.

I know I have a lot of fans in North Dakota. In fact, I probably have more fans than any golfer in the United States outside of Nicklaus. I hear from people all over North Dakota and around the country, and I really appreciate their encouragement and support.

Jim Adelson

Jim Adelson has been part of the sports world in North Dakota since 1952.

Minot residents recall those early years, when a brash young man with the heinie haircut burst onto the scene. He was an immediate hit with the listeners. Pop music fans twisted the radio dial to KCJB for Jim's popular radio program, and sports fans tuned in for his play-by-play broadcasts when the Mallards baseball team or the high school Magicians were in action.

Broadcast pioneer John Boler opened the first television station in North Dakota there in 1953, and Adelson made the transition to the small silver screen without missing a beat.

In 1957 a chance at the Big Time took Adelson to Binghampton, New York, where he rubbed shoulders with some of the stars of professional sports. He also sought out a golf instructor there who sharpened his game to what was to become championship calibre.

In 1961 Boler invited Jim to join the staff of KXJB-TV in Fargo. Jim's wife Barbara was anxious to return to North Dakota and, as he frankly admits, "The money was great." They came back.

Always ready with an opinion, a wisecrack or an inside scoop, the Waukegan, Illinois, native's style has made him one of the most discussed reporters in state history. Some viewers have become ardent fans. Others have taken a passionate dislike to the man...but one and all, they continue to watch him.

To describe Jim as outspoken or brash or controversial is only partly correct. He is a knowledgeable observer and a fine writer. He is also fair — though convincing some of the more maniacal fans of that can be a problem.

What's he really like? A lady asked him that question at a party once, and Jim replied, "Lady, I spit and I scratch and I don't like to talk."

I'll accept two-thirds of that.

My guest is one of North Dakota's most familiar faces and voices, sportscaster Jim Adelson. They are not only familiar with the face, Jim — they are familiar with the whole body.

When I say "one of North Dakota's most familiar faces," I think of your work in State Class A basketball and hockey and that statewide television hook-up through the KX stations. You probably have been seen across the state from east to west and from north to south more than any other sportscaster has. Is that safe to say?

I guess so. I have never thought of it that way, but I guess, when you get right down to the nitty gritty, I have been around a long time in everybody's living room, bedroom or whatever.

I have been asked many times over the years as your contemporary in sports broadcasting and also a good friend, "What is Jim Adelson really like?"

It's a cliche question, but there are people now who have only seen you on that little glass box or who have heard you on the radio who really do ask themselves that.

Are you the same off the air as when you are on the air? Do you change? Are you a comedian at all in daily life?

I don't think I'm any different. It's a legitimate question, though.

Back in my days in Binghamton, New York, I was at a party when a very attractive, very lovely woman came up to me and said, "Oh, I'm glad to meet you,"

I said, "Oh, really?"

She said, "Yeah, I have always wanted to see what you are really like."

I said, "Lady, I spit and I scratch, and I don't like to talk."

She looked at me kind of funny. . .but, no, I am outgoing, I like to have a good time, and I love people. I don't think I am any different on the air than I am off the air. At least, I try not to be.

OK, let's face it — you come across on the air sometimes a little flip, a little abrasive, a little on the outspoken side.

"Arrogant," too. I have heard a lot of words used.

All right, now, people might say that is part of your act, just to get people to watch — you know, "He says all those outlandish things so that we will tune in tomorrow." Is there any truth in that statement?

Might be. . .I think so.

A long time ago I decided how I was going to approach this thing. I was never blessed with the deep, stentorian tone of voice, so I thought, "Let's be yourself."

Some advertising executive told my mother once, "Tell Jim to just talk to people, and be himself." And I have tried to be that way.

That's why I have always admired your work, Boyd, because I think you have the same attitude.

I came into this market years ago against some very strong competition. I thought, "Maybe I should do it a little bit different." So I have tried to be a little fresh, express my opinions, make predictions — get half the town mad at me and the other half of town saying, "I hate that guy."

Then on Saturday night at a party they are saying, "Did you hear what that Adelson said? He is really a jerk." Somebody else will say, "Oh, now, wait a minute!" And they go on talking like this back and forth, and I am standing there saying to myself, "By God, they aren't talking about Terry Dean or whatever his name is on the other channel or Boyd Christenson."

I think I play the game well. I try to entertain people.

You once described the athlete as "an individual who has to have the body of a man and the heart of a boy." Might the same be said for Jim Adelson, sportscaster, to report on the games people play — have you got the body of a man and the heart of a boy?

I am not so sure I have the body of a man. . .

Yes, I think so, and I think it has kept me young. I love young people. I love their enthusiasm.

I think, too, Boyd, that I may not be the greatest sports announcer that ever came down the pike. I am not the kind of guy that is going to reach back and tell you what some guy's batting average was in 1953. But I am enthusiastic. I think, in every walk of life — no matter what you do — if you love your job and you're enthusiastic, you can overcome a lot of other deficiencies and you have it made.

Yes, I am a kid. I think I always will be. Even though I am fifty-four years old.

Let's talk about your relationship with other members of the media. You have been known to take a swipe at your contemporaries on the air. You used to have a running gun battle with Eugene Fitzgerald, God rest his soul — the former sports editor at The Forum. I know you loved him. But you cut him up one side and down the other side on occasion. There are a couple other writers who you take on from time to time, too.

Now, what is your relationship with those people after you have done this?

Well, there's one in particular in town who doesn't speak to me, but that really doesn't bother me. I have had a runnning gun battle with — I will mention this name — Eddie Kolpack (the current Forum sports editor), and Eddie and I are good friends. We laugh about it once in a while.

We really got mad at each other a couple of years ago. I had told him he was a lousy reporter, and he didn't talk to me for a while. But we mend those fences. I think relationships are pretty good with most of the other fellows.

North Dakota sports reporters each year elect the "sportscaster of the year." You have been in North Dakota for nearly thirty years. I have won the award, and so have guys in Devils Lake, in Wahpeton, in Grand Forks, in Williston and Minot. But you have never received this sort of recognition from your contemporaries. You must have some thoughts about that and about the award itself, don't you?

I think it all goes back a long time ago to one meeting where the vote was being taken. I got up and I said, "Why are we voting for ourselves?" I think it stinks. This is not a personality contest — who is doing the best job? Who knows what Boyd Christenson is doing in Minot, and who knows what Jim Adelson is doing in Minot. . .no one there even sees our work. Let's take an independent group and have them vote.

I got up in their meeting and I said this. I said, "It's stupid that we vote for ourselves," and some of the guys looked at me kind of crazy and said, "You are. . ." — well, whatever they said. I think that damaged my chances.

I got a little upset, too, because I know some stations were getting more ballots than they were entitled to. I know some guys were stuffing the ballot box.

I just said, "The hell with it. I am not going to vote."

It hurt me at first, because I knew I was doing a good job — at least, I thought I was, and I think you know whether you are doing a good job or not. But after a while, it didn't bother me at all any more.

I am mellowing out. But yes, it did bother me for awhile.

I have known you for a long while. We go back such a long way! I used to be a spotter for you in the press box during football games when I was a high school student and you were working in Minot.

So if I make this observation about you, not as a sportcaster but as friend off the air, I ought to have a pretty good feel for you: You have mellowed. What has contributed to that?

To be really honest, it was Barbara's death — Barbara, my wife. I lost her just a few years ago.

I was under an awful lot of strain when she was sick. I always have been kind of abrasive anyway, I guess; my former employer John Boler used to call me arrogant and quite a few other things, and I just guess it's just my manner.

But in coping with her illness and her death, I found out that there are a lot of things that are a lot more important these days than Jim Adelson. Since losing Barbara, I have given more of myself to other people and other things, my children, and I have mellowed a lot.

I think maybe I finally grew up. I miss Barbara very much at times, and I think that's sobered me up about life and about everything else.

She was a big fan. I used to see Barbara with you quite often in the press box. Was she also one of your severest critics?

Oh, yes. I can remember coming home many years ago when I was just starting to get the feel for television — it was in the beginning years; I think Bill Weaver was my competitor at that time on WDAY, and we only had two stations in Fargo.

I said, "By God, I knocked them dead! Everything went well. We had some good film and I talked well. I ad-libbed for about a minute and a half." We had long sportcasts then, six or eight minutes.

I said, "I was great. Did you see it?"

She said, "No, I was watching Channel Six. They had a good movie on."

Then she winked.

But, yes, she was a very severe critic. And I appreciated that. She was a hell of a woman. A great friend.

You have a family, a daughter and two sons. How has being in the limelight all over North Dakota affected your family? Their dad is the guy people see on television. Do you try to shield them from that?

You should answer that question yourself. You have been through this whole thing, too.

Well, it wasn't easy because I was and still am outspoken and say what I think on television.

Years ago when I was president of the North Dakota Sportscasters Association — I was the last one to be elected of all the group — well, anyway, I had to make the presentation at a Bison-Sioux basketball game at half time. We took Steven, our youngest, who was about ten or eleven.

There were about 10,000 people in the gymnasium. The announcer, said, "Now, your favorite sportcaster, Jim Adelson." I stood up and walked out on the floor. . .and ten thousand people booed.

Steven looked up at his mother and asked, "Why are they doing that?" And he started to cry.

I don't know. . .we have never tried to protect them. I think my children were always quite proud of the fact that their father was in the limelight. But at the same time, I can remember speaking at a pep rally at Fargo South High School, where all of our children went to school. Tom was a sophomore at the time.

After it was over I walked down the hall and ran into him. He said, "I heard you were good."

I asked, "Where were you?"

He said, "I was in the bathroom."

Our middle child, Tom, is a pretty good athlete and was always interested in sports. I took him to all the games and down to the station with me when I went to work — Steven, too — and I went to see both of them play whenever I could.

I went to see Tommy play basketball once when he was in the seventh grade. At that point we had great hopes — you know, this was definitely the proud father department. Good shooter, and he got in there, but he was too small, too slow — the coaches all said he was a smart kid, but he didn't get to play too much.

So he got into the game with about a minute to go. He brought the ball down, and he was dribbling. And of course all the guys hollered, "There's your dad." He looked over where I was sitting. The ball he was dribbling hit his foot and rolled out of bounds.

He could have died. I could have died. I didn't want to go to another game for a long time after that.

Do you think your sons, in particular, felt any pressure to go out for sports and excel in them because of who you were and what your job was?

They might have, and it wasn't easy for them.

Once when I was watching Tom, again, playing baseball when he was about eleven, the pitcher threw right at his head and said, "Here's one for the big TV star."

I think maybe they felt some pressure there, though I tried not to put it there.

Oh, I groomed my son Tom, you know. My wife was about ready to kill me because I threw hundreds of pitches left-handed. I made him bat both left-handed and right-handed. I wanted him to be the greatest baseball player that ever came down the pike.

Why?

I don't know. . .because I thought he had some talent, I guess. That was a bad mistake on my part — the jock syndrome at that time. He turned out to be a hell of a golfer. He quit baseball then.

Of course, he had one of the great teachers for golf, too — his dad was the North Dakota Senior champ a couple of times.

Well, I didn't help that much.

Were you a frustrated jock? I know your golf has been a tremendous source of pride for you, to win the seniors championship twice, and I know you wanted in the worst way to win an all-city tournament or to qualify for the Pine-to-Palm.

Why such a strong motivation? You had proven yourself in other areas. Was it a hangover from your school days, when you were a little kid, too small to make the teams?

I kind of think so.

My mother said I was born talking. . .I can believe that. I think your mother said the same thing about you, probably. Anyway, when I was a kid I was always up there talking all the time I played — "Here's Adelson, a great right-handed hitter."

When I was a kid I played in the park system, because that was where the kids with the worst hands were. I was a pretty good hitter, so I was a rare breed — it was usually the other way around.

And football — I had a heart murmur because I chased a girl one summer too hard. That is a true story, and why I couldn't play football. Her name was Barbara Green, as I remember — long blonde hair. Oh, how quickly we forget!

I think that's part of it, all right.

Golf — I have been obsessed with it! I just love the game. Just to get out there!

I am at the point where I can do things with the ball. I can't hit it very far, but I am a pretty good putter. And the fact that after all these years I finally won a tournament! Everybody said, "Luck," and they were right. You have to be lucky in sports — golf or in any game, And then the next year, when I stuck it right to them and won it again, they said, "Oh, my God, he really is a pretty good player. He talks about it and he can do it."

Oh, that was the biggest kick of my life!

And another thing — I am a very soft guy, though people don't know this. They are allowed to be embarrassed. But the greatest day of my life was when my son Tom and I played a match in the state tournament against each other.

I remember one of the first times you played a match against Tom. He showed up at the first tee wearing white earmuffs so he didn't have to listen to his dad.

Sure, that was the state tournament. We played head to head, and Barbara was alive then and over in the cart. . .

Let me interrupt for one second. I think that points up something about the fact that people make a game and a pastime of taking pot shots at you.

Here's your son who dearly loves you. You set yourself up for it beautifully — your own son comes up to the tee with earmuffs. You have set yourself up as fair game, in a way, for all the things people say and write about you. You are saying, in a way, "Come on guys, give me your best shot."

Oh, yes, even my own children!

But the great part of that story isn't done yet. After the third hole, I think, I was one up. You know, deep down you want the kid to win, you want the kid to succeed — but you still want to beat his tail if you can. I hit the tee shot and it went forty feet.

Tom hit one two hundred miles. He walked by me as I was shaking my head, and said, "Dad, you're swinging too fast."

I looked at him and I thought, "Here's this kid who wants to beat me so bad he can taste it, but yet he wants to help me, too. There must be some love there." I had tears in my eyes walking down the fairway.

You have done quite a bit of writing. You have a column in the "Midweek Eagle" and some other area newspapers. I've heard people say that Adelson is a much better writer than a sportscaster — that you should really stick to writing. What was your background? Were you trained as a journalist?

I was a sports editor of the "WTHS News," which is the Waukegan Township High School newspaper. I really wanted to be a sportswriter. I don't know — I thought that I wrote fairly well.

Then somehow after I went through the Army I got into the broadcast area. I am glad I did, because I'd have needed the detail part for a newspaper job, and it throws me.

I love to write. I hope someday to write a book. That sounds funny, but I do.

This "Midweek" thing started when they just called me up and asked if I would like to do it. I said yes. It's a challenge for me. I enjoy it. It's not the greatest but people have been very kind. It's a kick, and it's a way to get rid of some material. You know, with four minutes, you can't do much on the tube. It gives me a chance to expand on things,

Some years ago you left North Dakota after you had been here for, I suppose, seven or eight years. You went to Binghamton, New York, which I guess you could call the Big Time, for about four years. In our business that's common, moving from place to place.

Yes, it is.

Why did you come back to North Dakota from New York?

I came back, very simply, because a letter came from Mr. Boler and he said, "Would you come back?"

At that time I was terribly frustrated in New York. When I got the letter I called Barbara and said, "Do you want to go back to Fargo?"

She said, "When do we leave?"

Well, I think every young family with children is a partnership, and you have to ask them. If Barbara had said, "No, I don't want to go," I wouldn't have gone. But then, the money was great. At that time it was fantastic.

But let me ask you — are you one of these guys who have a big frustration that they never made it in what we call the Big Time?

At one time I was applying for a job announcing for the Chicago Cubs, and I guess I got to the semifinals. There were about ten of us after it there at WGN in Chicago, but I wasn't the one who got it.

That was a disappointment for you?

Terrible.

How about today? Do you feel that you are at a point in your career now where the Big Time is out and you are probably going to finish your career in Fargo? Do you think in those terms?

Either that, or maybe go someplace hot and play golf and do a little something on the side.

I don't know — I am happier now than I have been in a long time. I am doing some radio freelance work, as you know, and people have seemed to enjoy it. I am also doing a lot of different things on TV. We are doing bowling. The bowling show is just exciting for me. I'm having a lot of fun with it.

We do enough play-by-plays, too. Every sportscaster loves the play-by-play; you know that. I know that if there ever is one thing you have to miss, Boyd, it is the play-by-play. I am having such a good time with the people I am working with on the play-by-play and the kids.

I think, unless CBS would call and say, "We will give you a hundred thousand," there's nothing really to keep me in Fargo except some really good friends. My youngest son is graduating from high school and he is going to go away to school, and my other children are out of town.

You're talking like a man who maybe has some thoughts in the back of his mind about hanging it up.

Yeah? Oh, not for the next couple weeks, at least.

Oh, I think I am looking at five years from now, maybe. It depends on myself. Sometimes I think, "Gee, look at all these young guys scrambling around." There are some good-looking kids on the tube now competing against me.

I look at myself on tape every so often, and I say, "Oh, God, I can't stand the fat!" I play a lot of tennis and try to stay in shape.

I still have the enthusiasm. But the minute I think I am looking old and just don't have the enthusiasm, I think I will know. I hope to God there is somebody there, one of my dear friends, who will say to me, "Hey, kid, you know what — you've had it. Get off while you still can."

I loved Manny Marget. He was a great inspiration to me. But I don't think I want to be a Manny Marget, a guy who stays around forever.

You do have a boundless amount of enegy. You are doing some freelance sports with KFGO, play-by-play. You do play-by-play on KQWB. You have a column for the "Midweek Eagle." You do a call-in show on Sunday mornings as part of the Vikings games. You do two sportscasts a day. . .Jim, you do everything but sell jams and jellies in the lobby after concerts. You have a lot of good ideas.

Let me ask you — obviously, this must be fulfilling a need you have to do all this stuff. Do you like to work this much?

Yes, I love it. I guess I am a workaholic, and I play hard too. What you don't know is that in the summertime I play golf four or five times a week, too. But I do enjoy it, though I get awfully tired sometimes.

That call-in show on Sunday morning is the best one. I just love that, but it ends in January, you know.

I guess you just gear yourself to that life. I would be bored if I couldn't do them all. My days just fly by.

After Barbara died I had to do something, and I drove myself. But I have had some reversals, too, as in my history in business, and they put me in a bad position financially.

I was in the restaurant business for awhile and was also involved with a hockey team, and I lost my rear end. People were very cruel at that time. They just loved to watch it. It reminds me of when Roger Maris was going for the home run record in 1961 — how they bad-mouthed him and loved to see him get it.

Jim Adelson is some kind of a figure that people like to see fail. I heard a lot of people were glad I lost money. And I lost my tail. I had to do some things to get back, and pay some people back. I had a lot of debts.

That must hurt. But does that go back to when I said earlier in this conversation about your manner and your attitude on the air — that you set yourself up for shots? Sometimes people take some awfully hard shots, don't they? It has to hurt.

It does. I have tried to rise above it, but it can sting.

There's one sportscaster who came to town and he told me, "You know what, old man? I am going to beat your blankety, blank, blank, blank."

I said, "Who are you, kid?" Well, he hasn't. But I looked at him and I just thought, "Well. . .OK."

After a while you get awfully thick skin. I used to go home and cry once in awhile, maybe when I'd get a nasty letter.

You never got any, Boyd, because you were the all-American boy. God, I used to hate you on the tube! Everybody always said you were so cute, and you are — you are a very cute guy, have been ever since the days you used to spot with me for football. You did a lousy job but you were a nice kid!

We agreed earlier that you have probably gotten more state-wide exposure than any sportscaster in North Dakota television history. How many years did you and Channel Four do the state Class A basketball?

Twenty years.

You lost that contract last year, that one and the hockey. I know you enjoyed that, putting it on the air, and you were going statewide. That is gone now; another channel is going to be doing that for at least the rest of this year. What was your reaction to that?

As Charles Dickens wrote, "It was the best of times; it was the worst of times." Oh, hell — it was frankly the worst time of my life. I had lost my wife, and a month later I lost the state basketball tournament. You can't equate those, of course, but state basketball tournaments had been a part of my life for almost twenty years.

I got some bad press on it. I was misquoted, but I really did think that I deserved to keep it, and nobody had ever bid against us. Nobody ever competed against us to broadcast it, so I guess we took it for granted.

I would have thought that all the high school people had to do was let me know when there was competitive bidding. They never did, though they now say they did.

It is a bunch of bull. We spent twenty years building that tournament broadcast up to where, all of a sudden, all of the other stations said, "Hey, they've got a winner — let's grab it." And they had all the money in the world.

I was not thinking. Mr. Boler had let me make all the arrangements for twenty years, and I thought we'd been doing a good job. They caught me sleeping.

It was good business on their part, and I congratulate them — but they aren't going to catch me asleep again.

That was WDAY and KFYR television, the NBC stations. But now you turned around last fall and did football games on KQWB radio, coming away with the Bison football and basketball contracts that WDAY had held for about fourteen years. Suddenly the games are on another station and here's Adelson doing the play-by-play. Everybody's saying, "We knew Adelson would get even with those people somehow!" How much were you actually involved in that?

Not at all. Larry Lakoduk (owner of KQWB) is a good friend of mine. I had talked to him about this three or four years ago, when he'd told me, "I would sure like to establish something on KQWB-AM and show them we're something besides a juke box." He said, "If we get the Bison games, could you talk Mr. Boler into letting you do them?"

Nothing ever came of it. Then this fall Larry came around with the bid specs and asked me, "Are you still interested?"

I said, "Well. . ." We had lunch and I gave them some suggestions and some ideas and I said, "Well, good luck." Then I went off to play golf.

About three days later he called and said, "Guess what." And I fainted.

I have been accused of having something to do with opening that up. That is untrue. I am delighted that things kind of evened out, though.

I am not a bitter man. There are some people at the other station who think I set the whole thing up and I am telling you, with God as my witness, that I had nothing to do with it. But I am happy to be a part of it.

What is one of the most moving things that has ever happened to you — one moment that stands out, when you were really touched and you said, "Hey, I am in the right business — that is what it is all about"?

When we put the Fargo acro team on the tube, it was a very moving thing for me. They dedicated one number to my wife.

Another moment was in golf. I think it was the best thing in my whole life — when I won that North Dakota Senior golf tournament for the second time. After it was over, a very good friend of mine came over to me and said, "There are so many people so proud of you, and there is one who isn't here who also is terribly proud."

You know how I am, Boyd. I just broke up completely.

Lenus Carlson

I first met Lenny Carlson in 1966 when the young fellow from Cleveland, N.D., was a student at Moorhead State University and I was co-hosting WDAY-TV's "Party Line" in Fargo.

We were always looking for new talent to showcase on "Party Line." A viewer alerted us to "a young man at Moorhead State that you simply must hear sing." We did. . .and shortly after that, Lenny's performances became a regular feature on our program. He sang with us twice a week for the next two years.

I'm not suggesting that we discovered this great talent. We merely offered him the opportunity to use his magnificent voice and to polish the skills that would eventually take him to the Metropolitan Opera.

Seventeen Metropolitan Opera productions in seven years! That must rank you as a most successful opera singer.

I have been there quite often. . .probably more than some singers who are more famous than I am. But that's because it's my home base.

They picked me up right after college, as opposed to other alternatives that I might have had, like going to Europe, or trying to establish a reputation and a name for myself in American regional opera companies or the New York City Opera.

I was lucky enough to have worked with James Levine, who was the musical director at the Met. This was prior to his becoming the big gun that he is today. We had worked together, and so when he came in as principal conductor and later as the general director, he asked me to come over. I auditioned for the other directors, and they liked me.

I have had a fairly nice, easy ride of it, in terms of getting into the Met. Most people say, "Well, you don't get to the Met until you are forty."

It's been great.

Like they say, it's a long way from Cleveland, North Dakota. You were born in Cleveland, and educated in North Dakota and at Moorhead State University. Let's talk about those years right out of MSU: this gifted young man from North Dakota who has a magnificent voice sets out to try and crack the big time, so to speak.

There had to be some moments early on which, despite what you say about having had an easy time of it, weren't all that simple.

I was motivated all along to sing. When I came to Moorhead State, that's when I caught the opera bug. As you recall, Boyd, I tried to do opera once in awhile on WDAY, but I had a limited opera repertoire at that time so I sang mostly show tunes.

After I finished school, I spent one year in Minneapolis and made my living, sort of, as a singer there. I was with what was called Center Opera, now the Minnesota Opera, and made many local church appearances. I sang one very important engagement with the Minneapolis Symphony as a guest soloist. And then I was drafted.

I thought I had a choice. As it turned out, I didn't. I auditioned for the Army Chorus, which was a three-year gig. But at the time that I went in, which was June, 1968, they didn't have an opening there.

It was Catch 22. They said, "Okay, why don't you just go through basic training? By the time you get out of basic training, we will have an opening for you; you will get into the chorus, and we'll extend your period of time."

As it turned out, I spent twenty-one months in the Army as a clerk-typist. But I did maybe three or four opera productions with Colorado Springs Opera, where I was stationed.

You told me earlier that you had done some summer work in Central City in the Opera House.

Yes, those were my apprentice years. Each member of the musical performers' union I belong to was allowed two years of apprentice work. I did mine while I was in college. Most of the kids do their apprentice work now after they have finished their masters' degrees at twenty-six or twenty-seven years old.

Things have changed quite a bit. But I was lucky enough to get into an opera school where I got a great deal of experience, so that apprenticeship was not so important.

Artists and photographers carry around portfolios of their work — does an opera performer do the same thing, and assemble a portfolio of roles you are familiar with or are capable of doing?

Right. I have had an agent for years, and to a great extent he handles all of that.

I went to New York right after the Army in 1970, and I attended the Juilliard School of Music there for three years. While I was at the Juilliard School, I worked with Maria Callas, and that got a lot of attention for me. She got me my first job, my first official operatic debut — although my real operatic debut was certainly here with the Minnesota Opera.

What everyone likes to call my operatic debut with Callas, though, was in Dallas, Texas, where she was a great star. She had made her own American debut in Texas years before.

How did you come to the attention of Maria Callas?

She came to do a master class at Juilliard in 1971, and she wanted to hear the vocal students there. We all sang for her. She picked out a dozen; as it turned out, she used about three or four of us.

She taught two hours of master classes a week for eight weeks. There were talent scouts and people like Rudolph Bing, head of the Metropolitan Opera Company. The audience was filled with critics and all these famous people, and here we were, you know — just students, and singing for Maria Callas, no less.

I did well, fortunately, and got a lot of attention, and then my management came along. For about a year — let's say 1972 and 1973 and a little bit of 1974 — I did many auditions. I auditioned for European managers and most of the managements in America.

I got into the Met in 1974 and was on the radio. So consequently I think I have sung maybe only one audition since 1975.

That's great!

Yes, that is great. . .because I hate to audition!

Let me ask you about that first appearance at the Metropolitan Opera in 1974. How sharp is your memory? Can you take us back to two hours before curtain time?

I remember every moment of it.

They had been kind to me. In 1973 they had hired me to come to the Met to cover a performance — covering means understudying a performer. It turned out that I didn't have to go on, but it gave me a feel for the house. I got used to working with prompters and conductors and just to the space in the house — it's a huge opera house!

That was fortunate for me because, when I came back in 1974 to make my debut, I had a comfortable feeling in the house, at least. I made my debut as Silvio in "I Pagliacci."

Those were the last opera performances that Richard Tucker, the very famous American star, gave. We did five performances together that autumn, and he died just a month later.

It was a great, auspicious experience for me — to make my debut with Richard Tucker, the great Metropolitan Opera singer.

Did he do things to make you feel more comfortable?

Right. I had two weeks of rehearsal with him. It was a part that I had done before. I had done it in Dallas, as a matter of fact.

So I knew the part very well. But at any rate, I sang the part every morning, once through with my voice teacher. I vocalized every day for the whole two-week period. It was a really good build-up, a tremendous build-up.

One of the most painful things about getting ready for the debut was that the Metropolitan has open dress rehearsals. They are harder than opening night. Who comes to those open dress rehearsals? They're all the singers in town who want to see the opera for free. So out there are all these opera singers. . .one hundred fifty baritones! Once I got past the dress rehearsal — why, opening night was a piece of cake!

I was very nervous, you know, throughout the whole time period from the first day of rehearsal. It was a very nervous thing.

How do you relax? Nervousness, I assume, could affect your voice.

It does.

What tricks or exercises do you use, then?

That's an evolving thing. I feel that to a great extent I am not suffering from nervousness as much as I used to because of the technical expertise that I have gained through the years.

For one thing, you develop a certain amount of confidence in your technique because of experience in itself — you know, you have sung so many times.

My day goes like this. I tend to get up, oh, about ten o'clock and then take it easy — fool around, walk down to the Post Office, do things that involve getting a lot of air. Breathing exercise, you know. I sort of burn off that excitement right away when I get up, then have lunch and hopefully take a nap until four o'clock.

At four I start to get ready. I vocalize slowly, and then I eat at five and try to rest — you know, watch Mary Tyler Moore on TV or something like that to digest my food.

At six or six-thirty I start winding up my voice. When I walk into the opera house to put on my costume and make up for my eight o'clock show, usually it's boom! I'm ready to go. I always feel very good about that. That's when I get nervous.

Why does it disappear? What happens?

I don't know. When you're sitting there for thirty-five or forty minutes, depending on how long it takes, and you sit quietly. it just sort of all comes in on you — all the things that could go wrong.

But as soon as I get out of that chair, then I go and I run around the opera house. I am all dressed and have twenty minutes to walk around. And you can get a lot of exercise, because it's a big, big opera house. That walking sort of cools me down again.

Then the curtain goes up and there you are, okay again.

But you mentioned that you think of all the things that could go wrong. What kind of things have gone wrong when you have been on that stage?

Well, everything.

In my debut year — that was in 1974 — I did "Romeo et Juliette," with my role as Mercutio and Romeo played by Franco Corelli, the famous Italian tenor. We had a big fight scene, right? I am holding off Tybalt with my sword.

Everything in opera is said exactly in time to music, so your fight scenes have to last exactly that long before they are over. We had this all worked out. It was going easy enough

— boom, boom, boom, boom. Then Romeo is supposed to come running in and say, "Arretez" — you know, "Stop!" — and get in between us to hold us off. He subsequently goes about fighting him and I get killed.

Well, anyway, here I am sword-fighting with Tybalt — crack, crack, crack. The music stops, but Romeo is not back. My first performance, this is. No Romeo! All of a sudden, maybe ten beats late, you could hear him from 'way back there in the dressing rooms: "Arretez!" And he comes galloping onstage.

Everything came to a complete stop as he came running on, and then the opera could start again.

That's the perfect opening for the line, "Romeo, Romeo, wherefore art thou?"

The opera stars, men and women we see on TV and read about, seem to have tremendous senses of humor. They all seem to be very easy-going, light-hearted people. Is this approach necessary in your high-velocity business?

What happens to the superstars that you see on "The Johnny Carson Show" — and they are all quite big stars in constant demand all over Europe as well — is that they'll come in and rehearse a role on very short notice. They'll have maybe three or four rehearsals and go on.

So oftentimes they don't see the set or have an orchestra rehearsal. Frequently they just sit down with the conductor and run through it like the way we're talking right now.

And then boom! — they're on the stage with one hundred fifty people whom they have never seen before, and the star doesn't know where they all are going.

One of the great stories was in a production of "Un Ballo in Maschera," in the scene with the witch's brew. The witches were all around a big fire in a castle with a huge fireplace. The lady who had the starring role had arrived to sing the opera just that afternoon. . .and she made her big entrance through the fireplace!

This is just one of a thousand things that happen. They will walk off stage occasionally through a wall, you know. I have jumped in on too many occasions at the Met myself in an understudy situation where I was just praying to God that I was going to get through a scene.

You went on as an understudy, then? Had someone become ill or lost his voice?

Yes, one of my big breaks was as an understudy. It's happened twice, in fact.

I have jumped on seven times in all. Seven times! The longest notice was twenty-four hours, and the shortest was an hour and one-half.

I made my radio broadcast debut with an hour and one-half's notice, as Mercutio in "Romeo et Julliette."

What happened? Tell us about that.

I was covering a baritone who was a perfectly healthy guy, you know — I mean strong, and an excellent singer.

He got up Saturday morning for the Saturday broadcast feeling quite good. He went to the opera house at noon and something happened — he couldn't sing.

So they called me up at one-thirty. I had been singing a strenuous role night before, so I was really quite tired. I had never dreamed that I would have to go on. But they called me up.

I had gotten up late and I hadn't eaten, but I went running down there. I had to get a costume fitted and I had to work through the sword fights; I had never done the part before. Yet I went on and I did very well.

Somebody said that that's luck, but preparation had given you the opportunity. You obviously had prepared a long time for that break.

Yes, I have a tremendous fear of forgetting something or missing a cue or doing some staging wrong, so I go to great lengths to be well-prepared.

Where is your voice right now? Is that a fair question to ask an opera performer? Do you go through phases, transitions?

I have been cursed, so to speak, because I have a voice that has a rich undertone to it — a sort of bass undertone to it, and yet a tenorish quality at times. The management of those two things, combining them and blending them, has been a hard job.

I feel to a certain extent I am coming into my own now, after having studied singing for twenty years, really.

You have not yet reached your peak. . .is that what you are telling me?

No, not really. Furthermore, I haven't clearly established where I am best, high baritone or bass baritone.

Now, I think that it's characteristic of baritones that they don't mature until their late thirties, even baritones who don't have the sort of bass quality that I have.

So I am at a transition point in my career, definitely. I have made kind of a splash. I have made my debut in Covent Garden. I have sung in Europe; in fact, I sing in Europe every year. But at the same time I haven't pinned down the repertoire that I am going to ultimately be best at.

That's because I have been good at a lot of things. But I think that there's coming a time now for me at which I have to define that handful of roles that I might do as well as anyone has done. That's my job now. That's my dilemma, too.

That prospect sounds both exciting and frightening at the same time. Do you have some ambivalent feelings about this?

To be quite candid about the situation, I have had trouble establishing my repertoire in America. That's partly for the reason I have just mentioned — my range — but at the same time because in America we do so few performances.

There are thirty companies in this country. . .probably thirty, but maybe that's stretching it. . .with multi-million-dollar budgets. Going to Pittsburg or Houston or another regional company like that is a fine opportunity. You are there for ten days, and you do two performances.

But you don't know an opera until you have done twenty performances of it. So I can be busy working in this manner for ten years and still not have done twenty performances of the same role.

My problem right now, then, is to get that level of performance in. I am looking at probably having to go to Europe, stick with one of the better opera houses there and get my shot at fifteen or twenty performances of one specific role in a season. And then I could do my guest appearences elsewhere — see, that's the key. If I can do that and establish the fact that I can potentially do these parts very well, then my agent can sell me. He can say, "This is a performance that should be heard in the major capitals of the world."

But I have not done that. That's why Pavarotti is great. Pavarotti went to every great opera house in the world and sang one part. . .one part! He did two hundred performances in one year of "La Boheme."

So that's where you are right now in your career. . .

I have to define what I am good at, and make my name internationally with that. That is the next step.

You recorded an album back in 1967 when you had been appearing on "Party Line." It includes show tunes and some religious songs, and I still enjoy it. You told me earlier that you still go back from time to time and listen to this record and tapes of your singing of fifteen years ago.

Yes, and I have other tapes that are almost twenty years old.

Listening to your voice back at age twenty is not unlike looking at pictures of yourself twenty years later. You know, you see a certain shape of your face, a certain posture that you don't have any more but you remember from when you were young.

All right, so when I listen back to those recordings, they may be a year old or ten or fifteen years old. I listen for the changes that have been taking place. What qualities are coming into my singing now that were not there before?

There were some qualities before which, to a great extent, I didn't understand or appreciate. For example, there are some moments on the "Party Line" record that are equal to the best singing I have ever done — but they are only moments. They are relative to technical things, relative to my ability to communicate as a singer; they are relative to the beauty, just the simple, pure, natural, God-given beauty of the human voice.

I have to listen back to that once in awhile. I say to myself, "Look, you're giving a little bit more here than you need to, because it's cutting off a little bit from there." The voice at its most beautiful is long and fluent, and if you push up here, you lose there. If you push down from here, you lose something else.

In any case, your voice gets narrower in range, both range and tonal quality. So it's important to keep in touch with what is, for a singer, your basic instrument. Listening to those older recordings is how I do it. I was singing very well when I was in college, you know, quite naturally with good support and good placement. As a matter of fact, I am still studying with my same teacher, Duane Jorgenson.

. . .that you had in 1966?

Yes, at Moorhead State. He's at the University of Minnesota now. I come back and see him for a couple of weeks, and then I go off again.

What's your game plan, so to speak, for the near future?

As I said, I sing in Europe every year, but now I am talking about an extended period of time in the near future. That means giving up and going over there to live for a time.

Tomorrow I am going to judge the Metropolitan Opera regional auditions in Grand Forks, North Dakota. Twelve years ago, I was in those Met auditions myself.

And how did you do?

I won.

Agnes Geelan

Agnes Geelan is one of North Dakota's grand ladies. She's been involved in North Dakota politics and public life since before women got the vote, and has several "firsts" to her credit — first woman mayor and first woman state senator among them. She served in Bismarck under the William Guy administration in the Workmen's Compensation Bureau. She's been active in Nonpartisan League and Democratic politics for some fifty years.

After her retirement in 1975 Mrs. Geelan set out on another new career, that of a writer. Her book was **The Dakota Maverick**, *a political biography of William Langer.*

You've just completed your second literary effort, Agnes, at the ripe young age of eighty-five, and I understand it's a complete departure from the Langer book, which was such a success in North Dakota. What's the new one about?

It is different, Boyd. The Langer book was based on a great deal of research I did on his public life — hundreds and hundreds of interviews of people who knew him, and hours and hours in libraries researching his papers and articles written about him.

This new one is a novel, and I'll tell you how that came about. When I was first working on the Langer book almost ten years ago, a friend who was an author herself gave me the best advice. She said, "If you're going to write a book, you're just going to have to write something every single day."

Well, you know, that was tough — writing every day. But after a while it got easier. Then it got to be a habit! So after the third edition of the Langer book was published and sold out, I started writing again about things that interested me.

But I had a problem. How was I going to get people to read this? It was no task to get them to read the Langer book because he's so well-known to people around North Dakota, probably the most famous figure in our state's history.

I had to find a way to work all the topics I was reading and writing about into some form that people would enjoy reading. That's why I decided to weave it into a cloth that would depict life in a small midwestern town.

I'm a product of small towns. I was born in Hatton, then I went to college in Mayville, and I taught in Lankin, Oberon, Mayville and Enderlin for eighteen years. So I know something about small town society and wove a fictional plot around it.

Is it set in North Dakota?

No, I created a fictitious Minnesota town called Pine Cove.

Now, the reason I chose Minnesota was that I became interested in the Chippewa Indians when I was writing about Bill Langer, so I had to choose a location near theirs.

Langer's father bought Indian scrip land when he arrived in North Dakota. I wondered about that: what is it? So I got a copy of the treaty where eastern North Dakota and western Minnesota were ceded to the United States government by the Chippewa Indians.

Also, Mr. Geelan and I had a summer place on the Ash River in Minnesota — lo and behold, another tract of land that the Chippewas had ceded to the United States. I got that treaty, too. Reading the two of them, I became interested in the Chippewa people. I later became close to some of them in our church parish.

All of this is only a subplot in the novel, but one character is a Chippewa Indian girl and another shows this same interest as mine in their history.

So, although it's fiction, the person of Agnes Geelan shows up in the book every now and then.

It's a little hard to keep yourself out of it! They tell me that when you write fiction, you always get parts of yourself into it, and many parts of my life did find their way in there — my experience with a fraternal order, for example, which in the book I call the Ancient Order of Penguins.

The only thing that's definitely not in there is that I didn't include any of my political experiences.

What's the book called?

The Ministers' Daughters.

We'll be looking forward to it.

You've done so many things in your lifetime that I hardly know where to begin. In many different positions, though, you've been the first woman to have achieved one goal or another. I know you also served on the original Commission on the Status of Women, which twenty years ago was studying many of the problems that women are still working to solve today. How did you become involved in that organization?

I was serving on the Workmen's Compensation Board at the invitation of Governor Guy in 1964 when he appointed a committee to make recommendations for later study of issues relating to equal treatment of women and men in North Dakota. We studied the laws and made our report to the governor and then disbanded. The present commission was reactivated some ten years later.

What was the group like? How did your concerns then compare with the issues that are controversial today, like the Equal Rights Amendment?

I've never worked with a more wonderful group of women . . . Brynhild Haugland, Sybil Kelly, Anna Powers, Elvira Jestrab. We had two men, too, Askew from Bell telephone and Wally Dockter of the AFL-CIO. We all had strong and differing political convictions, but we never had a bit of political discussion or dissension keeping us from our task.

The Equal Rights Amendment wasn't coming in for much discussion then, back in the middle 1960s, but we made recommendations on similar kinds of things — state laws that segregated women or were discriminatory. One was the minimum wage, for example, that was lower for women than men. Another was the jury law.

We concentrated on our state laws. We had no appropriation and had to beg money to print our report, even to mail it.

Really, when you look back at it, we made some good recommendations that were ahead of their time. Some haven't even been satisfied today. The report guided the next Status of Women Commission when it was formed under Governor Link.

Your political involvement goes back to the old days when the Nonpartisan League was just being formed in North Dakota. Wasn't the NPL your first political affiliation?

No, my husband Elric and I called ourselves Democrats. The Republicans were very much in control of the state in those days, after the first success of the League had begun to fade, and it was part of the Republican Party.

I was mayor in Enderlin at the time the Nonpartisan League was reactivated after the 1947 Legislature met. Do you remember that session, Boyd? It was Republican from top to bottom. Lloyd Omdahl called it "the careless majority." It showed a very decided anti-Farmers Union bias and passed some laws that were definitely anti-labor.

After it adjourned, the Farmers Union and labor organizations decided they needed to reactivate the Nonpartisan League to fight for what they believed in. The labor boys in Enderlin told me, "You've got to go to the convention as a delegate," and then, "you've got to help reorganize the League in Ransom County."

And then they conceived an impossible thing: they decided I should run for Congress.

That would have been in 1948.

That's right. And to everybody's surprise, I was endorsed to run with Usher Burdick.

That was my start in state politics with the Nonpartisan League.

You ran for Congress again in 1956, didn't you?

Yes, but quite a few things had happened in between!

While I was serving as mayor of Enderlin I was elected state senator. That was in 1950. While I was in the Senate I got interested in the "insurgent movement." the group of younger NPLers who ultimately were able to move the League from the Republican column into a merger with the Democratic Party.

I was in the 1951 and 1953 sessions of the Legislature but I lost in 1954 when I ran for reelection. The truth of the matter is that I was just defeated by the better candidate, Don Holand. He went on to the Senate and did a tremendous job. . .so I've always got to admit I was beaten by the better man.

It's not too often a politician will admit that!

Well, I've always been a realist. Ever since then I've been ready to admit that the people of Ransom County didn't make a mistake when they sent Don Holand to Bismarck.

After I was defeated, though, I was appointed to the executive committee of the NPL. We worked hard and, in 1956, the League endorsed its first full slate of candidates running in the Democratic column on the ballot. And again, I was the candidate for Congress.

You've been the first woman in North Dakota to achieve all kinds of things in politics and public life. How do you feel about women in the political arena? Do women candidates start with a couple strikes against them here in North Dakota?

Not a bit. Not one bit, Boyd. North Dakota has been very, very good to woman candidates.

When you go back even to the 1890s, before women could vote or hold state offices outside of the Superintendent of Public Instruction, two women were elected to that job. Then there was Berta Baker. She was invincible!

Or look at Fargo and Cass County — women city and county commissioners, women school board members, women legislators who run near the top in every election.

No, I have never found any bias against women, not even in the German counties that are supposed to be so conservative or anti-women. When I ran with Dr. Bertel Hocking in 1956 for Congress, he said I'd be slaughtered there. I didn't believe him and I wasn't. I got more votes than he did in every one but one of them!

Did you enjoy campaigning, making speeches and shaking hands?

Oh, my, yes, very much. I enjoyed it because for the first time I saw how indebted we are, as candidates, to the people. People work tirelessly for you, even those who really have no thought of getting patronage. They're just working because they want to see you elected.

You know, Boyd, it's truly thrilling.

What prompted the merger between the NPL and the Democrats back in 1956? That has turned out to be one of the most important dates in our recent political history.

We should never have been in the Republican column. Understand, I'm talking as a Democrat now. I'm talking as a liberal in the League tradition. It was all right as long as the Nonpartisan League controlled the Republican Party and could keep the philosophy and platform liberal. But somewhere along the line it got to be conservative.

The choice was really in the primary, then, between the League candidate and the ROC (Republican Organizing Committee) endorsee; the winner would be the Republican name on the ballot in the general election. As the Republican Party got more conservative, the ROC candidate usually won the primary.

What happened then was that we voted Nonpartisan League in the primary election but ended up voting Democratic in the fall. We should for many, many years have been in the Democratic column, and in 1956 we finally made it.

Of course, we were all defeated in 1956. Even Quentin Burdick was defeated that time, running for the U.S. Senate. I always have remembered, though, what Ervin Schumacher wrote me after we'd both lost in 1948: "When you build a foundation, somebody has to be the gravel."

I don't think any of us regretted being the gravel because, of course, by 1960 we had the first real two-party system in North Dakota history.

Tell us about your experiences in that campaign.

Quentin Burdick was running for the United States Senate in 1956 while Dr. Hocking and I were running for the House.

What kind of campaigner was Senator Burdick?

Excellent campaigner, just the same as he is now. He'd go down the street of those little towns in his rumpled suit and shake hands with everybody. He didn't call everyone by their first names as Bill Langer did, but everybody knew Burdick, so he didn't have to introduce himself. Most people knew what he looked like.

How about his father Usher, who preceded him in the Senate?

Well, I campaigned with Usher, too, of course. Usher and I were the nominees in 1948. He was something else again! He campaigned just exactly like Langer — putting his arms around everybody, calling most of them by their first names, driving miles out of his way to stop and see some farmer and talk to him.

Did it ever dawn on you, during those days when you were in the ring with some of the state's most interesting political battles, that you might someday be writing about Langer yourself?

Never. In the first place, I didn't think I was a writer. And I don't call myself that yet.

But I waited and waited for somebody to write the real story on Bill Langer, and nobody else came forward to do it. There was Holzworth's book **The Fighting Governor**, but that was just written as campaign material. Langer was running for the Senate at the time. While some of my critics have accused me of being too good to Langer in my book, in Holzworth's he could simply do no wrong!

My interest in Langer continued over the years I served in the Guy administration and was a delegate to the state Constitutional Convention. But I retired from the Workmen's Compensation Board at seventy-five so that no one could say Bill Guy had a senile old woman in his administration, and I came back to Fargo.

I'd been unfortunate enough to lose my dear husband before that, so there I was — a seventy-five-year-old widow who was out of a job. I decided that, well, I'll go back to school and see if I can put enough sentences together to try to write a book.

You came back to North Dakota State University then, in 1971, you've said, to learn how to write. Tell us about how you got started there.

I'd earned my teaching certificate more than 50 years before, you know, but I thought I might want to finish my degree.

I took all the English courses that I could take, and one was a very fine basic course taught by Mrs. Alice Dickey. She was an excellent instructor, but I knew that what I was handing in was just terrible.

Then one day she gave us an assignment that made me realize what I'd been doing wrong. She said, "Write about the most interesting thing you saw or read or thought about today. Forget about writing, and write like you think."

That day she'd walked into our class — it was summer — wearing shorts and smoking a cigarette. So I wrote what a woman I'd known on the Enderlin school board would have done if in 1930, when I was teaching there, I'd walked into a schoolroom wearing shorts and smoking.

And so I learned the most important lesson for writers, which is to write as you think. . .write as you talk.

How did you find the material you used for the Langer book?

I interviewed literally hundreds of people. I started out with a list of just one hundred. Everywhere I'd go, they'd say, "Oh, you must interview this one, too. You must talk to that one." So it got to be many hundreds before I was through, and I could have interviewed thousands if I'd pursued it.

Why hasn't more been written about this powerful figure in North Dakota politics?

That's what I could never understand.

Now, this isn't a definitive, complete biography. To do that, I'd have had to continue my research for ten or fifteen or twenty-five years more. All I attempted to do, Boyd, was to portray Langer the politician as I and the hundreds I talked to saw him.

I used to hear politicians say that no one was lukewarm about the man. Either you loved him or you hated him. Did you talk with people on both sides?

Indeed I did. Since he died only in 1959, I interviewed people who'd been his enemies during his lifetime. Many of them never mellowed a bit in their feeling toward him.

Just the other day someone told me about a man in Devils Lake who carries my book around so that he can show people that I have him listed as one of the petitioners who tried to keep Langer out of the Senate. He's proud to this day.

You've mentioned that you believe Langer was a man ahead of his time. Why do you say that?

He was a man fifty years ahead of his time. Today many of the things he supported don't seem so outrageous as they did in his time.

He was, for example, an early and ardent supporter of the Equal Rights Amendment. In 1943 a resolution came out of his Senate Judiciary Committee giving a favorable do-pass recommendation to the Equal Rights Amendment. Even before then, during the year and three months between when he was elected and when he was seated, he got letters from some clubwomen in Rugby asking him to support the amendment. At that time he wrote back and said, "I'll do everything I can." I came across the letters in his correspondence in the University of North Dakota library.

Another interesting item in your book — he was an early advocate of finding ways to replenish our dwindling fuel supply.

That was one of the first bills he introduced in the Senate, even before he was seated. It was in 1941, and was "to establish plans for the manufacture of power fuel from agricultural products and lignite, to help solve the gasoline shortage." That's thirty or forty years before the United States caught up to him with the Arab oil embargo, coal gasification, gasohol and so on.

He was a forward-looking man, then, but much maligned. What's the reason behind that?

He was a wheeler-dealer, there's no question about it. And then, he was a liberal. . .and we have quite a few people in this state who aren't exactly liberal. In fact, I asked one newspaper editor to see the last editorial he'd written on Langer. I said, "Surely you wrote something good about him when he died."

He said, "What was there good to say?"

Of course, your title tells part of the story. He truly was a maverick politician, elected as a Republican but voting with the Democrats most of the time.

The Congressional Almanac each year lists the five worst senators and representatives, along with the five best, in terms of their loyalty to their parties. Langer was always among the five worst and was usually the first worst.

Why choose to do that? Why didn't he run as a Democrat?

Because he would have lost some of his Republican rights by changing parties. And then, of course, he stayed with the Nonpartisan League. Until nearly the end of his career that meant he ran in the Republican column on the North Dakota election ballot.

He was a maverick, but he was first, last and all a Nonpartisan Leaguer. However he voted, he was voting his convictions.

But how could he get by with that?

I included some pretty scathing things in the book that his fellow Republican senators said about him. They asked him why he didn't go over to sit with the Democrats on the other side of the aisle, and they blocked some of his appointments even when he sat on the governing committee. Oh, yes, Langer had his enemies. But he was nevertheless a powerful figure in his own right.

Let's touch on some of the other prominent politicians you've known. How about William Lemke?

When I was first endorsed for Congress with Usher Burdick, Lemke and Robertson were endorsed by the ROC, so I campaigned against him — my very first start in North Dakota politics. You can imagine how much chance I had against Lemke! He was running then for his seventh term, Robertson for this third, and Burdick for what would have been his fifth. So what in the world was Agnes Geelan doing in that campaign?

What kind of platform did you run on in 1948 and again in 1956? What were you promising the folks?

I didn't make too many promises, but I was true to the platforms of the times. One big thing was that we were asking for a better farm program. I had to sit down and talk with some farmers until I got educated on what a good farm program meant. We believed, of course, in Social Security, which was just coming in. I would say that they were very typical Democratic platforms.

Usher Burdick went on to a parting of ways with the Republican Party, too, did he not?

That was at the endorsing convention in 1958. He was Congressman then, but they didn't even recognize him from the floor. He was too liberal for many of the Republicans.

They didn't endorse him for reelection, and he went away in disgust and gave his blessing to his son Quentin, who ran for his seat as the Democratic-NPL candidate. Many people have said that the only reason Quentin was able to win Langer's Senate seat after his death was his two years of experience in the U.S. House. As close as his race was with John Davis in 1960, I doubt very much that he'd have won without his victory in 1958.

The Republicans had lost the Nonpartisan League in 1956 — that was Langer, you see — and then they didn't elect their own to the House in 1958, so ultimately they lost two Senate seats in that one election.

Recently Arthur Schlesinger wrote in a national publication that politics goes through periodic swings — first liberal, then conservative, then liberal again — every fifteen or twenty years. In your own years of participation in the political process, have you observed the same thing to be true?

Yes, indeed I have. The Nonpartisan League was originally effective in North Dakota because of its liberal, populist philosophy, and then lost power when the state swung over toward a conservative view. We've seen that time and again in North Dakota. It's part of our history as well as our nation's.

You were on the Democratic platform committee, were you not, during another of the nation's periodic swings toward liberalism in 1960. It's just two decades ago, but already part of history. What kinds of things was your party talking about then?

About the same things we're talking about now, Boyd — better farm programs, for one thing. The Soil Bank program came in for quite a bit of discussion back then, like PIK now.

Then, of course, there was Jack Kennedy with his liberal philosophy. Mrs. Roosevelt was there with us, and a lot of the talk was of the old liberal Franklin Roosevelt approaches.

Were you impressed by Jack Kennedy?

Oh, yes, very much so.

What was the feeling at that convention like?

Kennedy was a charismatic man, no question about it. That made it quite an interesting convention. Our North Dakota delegation was instructed to vote for Hubert Humphrey, until he gave up his quest for the presidency that year. We were in quite a bind there. It was just at the very last that North Dakota went for Jack Kennedy.

You were part of the state delegation to two important conventions, 1956 as well as 1960. What were those groups like? Were you unified?

We were not. When I went to the Chicago convention in 1956, Abner Larson and Rosamond O'Brien actually walked out of our delegation when we supported Adlai Stevenson.

We weren't particularly unified in 1960, either. A lot of people worked for Hubert Humphrey right up until the very end.

I don't think we've ever been truly unified, Boyd. That's one of the great things about North Dakota as well as the Democratic Party. We're always so independent in our views.

Critics frequently disparage strict party politics. You remember Will Rogers' old saying, "a yellow dog Democrat," meaning that Democrats would vote for their party's candidate if they ran a yellow dog, as long as he was Democrat. How fair is that criticism, Agnes?

Most of the time, I suppose, it is fair.

Let's take myself. Most of the time I would say yes, you should support your party and its people. I only know of one instance where I couldn't vote for the nominee of the Nonpartisan League. It takes something drastic for me to abandon my party's choice, but I could see where I couldn't support a certain candidate for the presidency.

But if you don't support your party, you're just about half a party member. I believe we should stay loyal. That's how we accomplish things in our system.

In other words, we need the political parties for a base of support — a springboard. Obviously that means some compromises are in order.

Oh, now that's one lesson I learned, Boyd, in the state Senate. I suppose I started out a flaming wild-eyed liberal. I thought everything was a matter of black or white, and that we had all the answers.

In that session I really learned the lesson of political tolerance. Most good legislation is a result of the art of compromise.

Fritz Scholder

Fritz Scholder is, quite simply, the most organized artist I have ever talked with. He's organized in the sense that he knows what he wants to do and say, and lets nothing interfere with the finished product: his magnificent paintings.

During our conversations at the Plains Art Museum — where his work was the subject of a much-admired one-man show — he described himself alternately as a rebel. . .a loner as an artist. . .an egomaniac. . .a breaker of the rules. . .and "not an Indian in any way," although he is invariably described in print as "Fritz Scholder, noted Indian artist."

Scholder's is one of my favorite television conversations. Viewers saw an intelligent and gifted man, which he of course is. On occasion an interviewer can get in the way of a conversation and actually become a barrier in the line of communication between guest and audience. That was never the case with him — but, then, whether Fritz Scholder is painting a picture with his brilliant colors and a brush or with words, he simply pushes any barriers aside.

Do you really believe, as you've been quoted saying, that where someone comes from is important in his work?

I think it's terribly important, because one has to find one's own identity. A great deal of that has to do with where one comes from.

I was born in Breckenridge, Minnesota, and I grew up in Wahpeton, North Dakota, spent the first fourteen years of my life there.

You have also said that you came from, in your phrase, "a non-Indian cultural setting."

I grew up in a very non-Indian environment. My father was educated at Indian schools and was taught well to become white. And so he, being half Indian, really pretty much existed in the non-Indian world. He was president of the Rotary Club and did a lot of things that anyone would do in this area.

Yet you're referred to, even in your own news releases, as "Fritz Scholder, noted Indian artist." Everybody speaks of you that way, I guess because we all have an urge to categorize people. But you don't consider yourself an Indian artist at all.

No. I am not an Indian in any sense of the term.

First of all, one can't be an Indian if one is only one-quarter Indian. I am German, French and English.

I am very proud of being one-quarter Indian but I am not in any way an Indian.

Fritz, you have said that art is making people reevaluate their ideas. Is that a difficult task for you, considering that the art we see today depicting the Indian is so highly romanticized?

I think that's the main challenge for any artist, for any subject, because today everything is visually cliched. . . landscape, still life. . .and so it's the task of the artist to in some way present a new visual experience.

With the invention of the camera, you see, the role of the artist changed.

So you stepped in to fill a void?

I think every artist does this, yes. When I do a painting of a dog, it has to be a dog of which I think people will say, "Scholder painted that." I think that, believe it or not, after you see a few dogs of mine in my paintings, you will be able to recognize them a mile away.

In your early work you did a number of landscapes, and you once vowed that you would never paint the Indian. Obviously something happened to change your mind.

It was when I happened to get a job in Santa Fe — my first and only full-time job, teaching at a new Indian art school. When I came to Santa Fe, I saw everyone was painting the Indian, and I vowed I would not. I am essentially a rebel, and I never do what everyone else does.

More than that, all of these painters were painting a very romantic version of a very loaded subject, and I really didn't want any part of it.

But later, by teaching young Indian artists and going to the Indian dances and collecting Indian artifacts, I became very interested in the subject. I realized that no one had really approached the subject in contemporary terms and in terms that conceivably were real.

Can we talk about that a little more? Fritz, you say you were a rebel. Let's talk a little more about what, exactly, you rebelled against.

Well, I have always felt like an alien wherever I was.

I am the type who will never just accept somebody else's statement. I have to find out for myself.

I always knew that what I wanted to do was to paint, for instance. This was at a time when no one was making a living at painting in this country. The syndrome was that you had to go to Paris and starve in a garret. But early on, I knew that this is what I wanted.

The artist in me is a loner. I work alone in the studio. As an artist, you do things that you realize not everyone is going to like, and so you can't worry about that. You have to just do what you have to do. Believe it or not, some of my paintings have been described as controversial, and still are to some people

But of course painting is very personal. Somebody might object to a pink sky: you can't worry about it. You are the artist and you can paint that sky any color you want.

It must be an upsetting and exciting time for an artist — that point when he becomes accepted, even famous. It's almost as if he has arrived and his point of view has won out.

It's always nice to realize that some people can connect with what you are doing and come on your wavelength. I come halfway by painting a picture, and the viewer has to come the other half. If they can't come that half, that's their problem, because I have done all I can.

I don't say everything in the work. There are some things that people should conceivably wonder about. There should be areas of mystery.

I am not literal. Art is of course a way of communicating somewhat of a concept. It is good in that it forces people to reexamine and reevaluate their ideas on a work's subject, or just on the subject of painting and how paint is applied, how color is used.

People, in fact, have been talking to me about never really seeing color used in this way. For some of them, I think that maybe it is opening their eyes to a new color sense.

I like the old Japanese saying, "Have you ever seen a flower garden that clashed?" Any colors can be used together. Now, one color by itself isn't that interesting. When you get that second or third color next to each other, then things start happening.

People look at your work and they assume that Fritz Scholder and his painting are making a statement of some kind. But you say you are not making a statement.

Well. . .I deny consciously making a statement, but of course I am.

Here's part of a paradox — my favorite word, because when you look at anything in any depth, you realize that it's a paradox. You can say one thing and then turn around and say the other.

I do deny making any statement in the work because I don't like to talk about the work itself. I talk around it. The work is visual; people can approach it on whatever level they choose, and its meaning depends on their frame of reference. That's what they are going to get out of it.

But the work is, in a way, esoteric. It has to be. It's very personal, and I know it won't be understood by everyone who sees it. I did it, but I have gone as far as I can go with it, and that's all that I am going to do.

Can you share with us the feelings that your art evokes for you, whether in the first moment you stepped up to the blank canvas, midway or at completion?

For me, the real joy of painting is the actual act. It's a very sensous activity. You have a flexible brush and buttery paint and color, and the canvas moves when you touch it.

That does sound sensual.

I work with loud rock music playing. Pretty much I work in a trance. I love the whole activity and the experience.

Once it's done, I divorce myself because then it goes into a whole different realm — the realm of the viewer, the collector, the entrepreneur, the publisher, on down the line. . .and I am on to the next painting.

Right now I am terribly excited about the paintings that are still in the studio that I left behind. I come into this gallery (the Plains Art Museum) and look at these paintings in their exhibit of my work almost as if they were strangers. I wonder who did them.

You work with extremely large canvases. You've said that with a large canvas, you can either have a large triumph or a large mess.

Exactly. These are taller than I am, wider than I am if I stretch my arms. With them, you have an entity in the studio with you. It's almost a battle with the canvas, and you know, I like it that way. The large ones are, I think, the luxury of painting.

Although it depends. There are times when I feel very much in the mood to do the small canvas. In a way, a small canvas is very difficult, also. To do a small canvas and make it powerful is a feat.

Going back to either the big triumph or the big mess, people assume that somewhere in every artist's quarters is a little back room that is padlocked, containing the ones that didn't work out. Is there such a place in your home?

There were many years in which I really did cover over many painted canvases or slash them. But paintings require a maturing process. The more you paint, the better you really do get, and now I pretty much know how to make it work.

It's strange. About five years ago I was in the studio working on a canvas and it just wasn't coming along like I wanted. I was getting very frustrated. All of a sudden something hit me and — this won't sound like much because it's one of those things that are either right for you or not — but the idea hit me that I couldn't make mistakes! There was no way because it was my canvas. It was. I was doing it, and if I didn't like a certain brush stroke, I could cover it or scrape it off. If I didn't like it, I could paint over it. It was really only up to me.

And somehow that really hit me. I thought that it was a revelation. And so in the last five years I really have felt my power.

You say that the artist has to learn the rules before you can break them. How did you learn the rules yourself?

Actually, I learned the rules, a great many of them, here in this area. I was fortunate in my freshman year to go to Wisconsin State University in Superior. A number of my teachers were Bauhaus people, so I had a very strict background. . .which I found most helpful when I landed in California.

Are you about to break some old rules? You've mentioned that you have two pieces now that you are working on which are a little more abstract than Scholder fans have become accustomed to. Are you going to surprise some people with your next canvases?

I am always breaking rules. That's part, I think, of living.

The new canvases are more abstract. It will be much more difficult for people to understand them. One has to push oneself as well as the viewer. I'm my own worst critic.

One can't be stagnant. One can't paint the same thing over and over. Once it's done, it's done, and you have to continue onwards.

That's why I like to also experiment with different art forms. I am now doing sculpture, and I'm very excited about that. I have been doing monotypes recently, and they've become a very important part of the work.

You mentioned that as an artist, you have to work in a controlled environment. How do you maintain control of your environment?

The environment is something that can't be denied, I think, by anyone. The world around you has some influence on your work.

The studio environment is, of course, very controlled. When I walk into my studio, I'm almost like Pavlov's dog. I am conditioned to work. I never know what is going to happen next — that is part of the joy of it. It's a matter of walking in there, with canvases stretched and waiting for me. I can start immediately whenever I want.

Is there a time of day when you are more productive?

I guess when I taught I became a night painter. I still do a lot of painting at night. But I am very undisciplined. I go into the studio and I get too nervous to do anything else. I really don't go into the studio that often.

I have a friend who is a poet, a very good poet, who said that early on in his career he made a rule that he would never take any suggestions for poems from his wife, from any of his children or from any of his close friends. How about in your situation?

Someone did say that the worst enemies are your family and friends. But on the other hand, I do like to get another reaction because one becomes too close to the painting to see it objectively.

Usually when I finish a painting, if Ramona is around, I call her in immediately just to get another reaction.

Is she a good critic?

Yes.

You value her opinion?

Well, now, that's interesting. I listen to her reaction, you know, but then I have to weigh it in regard to what I was interested in as I was painting it. One has to take responsibility.

But there are times when a fresh eye will see something, conceivably, that maybe I wasn't aware of.

You said, "I am not worried about what people think. I have done the best I can do." You are obviously, from that statement, a very confident and well-adjusted rebel, as you've told us you think of yourself.

Yes, I really am. I am an egomaniac. I think a painter who is worth anything must be because, you see, what you do is completely done by you. No one is behind you in the studio whispering in your ear what color to put on next. So when these things are done, I have to stand and say, "I did it."

I am very pleased to stand next to a work that I have decided to let out of the studio and say, "I did it."

One of my favorites among your paintings is "American Indian" — the Indian with the stripes and the stars and the red, white and blue. Now, you can't tell me you weren't making a statement of some kind there!

I certainly was not making any statement. It's interesting that you question me about that particular one, too, because so many people have read so many things into it.

One of my favorite stories is that when it was hanging in one of the museums in the East, a lady came up and looked at it and said, "Well, finally, a patriotic Indian."

Actually I did that painting that way because I ran across some research which was very interesting. Around 1880 the government sent surplus flags to the reservations for no good reason. . .something like the government usually does. The reservations didn't know what to do with them, so they handed out these flags to some of the old chiefs. They immediately saw the design possibilities and incorporated them into their own regalia. You can in fact find photographs showing some of these old chiefs wrapped with flags. You see, often fact is much stranger than fiction.

I have always tried to portray every subject in some kind of reality. With the Indian, really, the fact is so strange that you don't have to make up anything. When I did "Indian in Paris," the Eiffel Tower was in the backgrouond, and some people undoubtedly wondered why I'd painted him in Paris. Was I just making it up? Buffalo Bill brought his Wild West Show to Paris at the turn of the century and lined them up in front of the Eiffel Tower and took photographs of them.

All I have done is try to set the record straight on any subject — tried to in some way find the real cowboy, the real Indian, or the real dog or whatever.

But you have said, "The Indian must learn to leave the arena of cliches, the trading post and the trinkets," I assume you are referring to their art. Have you seen this happening at all? Has your work been influenced in that regard?

I guess so. It is paradoxical. Although I am not an Indian, I happen to have started a series on American Indians at a time that was very receptive. I also have been influential to many young Indian painters because of that.

That influence is something that I am proud of, really, because it was a positive thing. You see, until 1960 the Indian artist did not have the freedom really to paint the way he wanted. If he didn't paint a certain flat style, the trader couldn't sell the work and wouldn't buy his goods, even at the very low sums that were being paid at the time. It was really kind of pitiful. Any Indian person who wanted to be an artist found himself in that trap.

It wasn't until the 1960s that it changed, and part of that was because of the hippie movement. Indian people realized that here were non-Indians dressing up like Indians, very taken with the costumes and even concepts and philosophy of Indian culture.

Finally the American Indian artist broke out of the stereotypes. I guess I was perhaps the first one to break out of all that into a kind of abstract style, because already I was being labeled as an American Indian artist. Many others followed suit.

And so today Indian artists are doing all kinds of things, which I think, generally speaking, is healthy because every artist has to have that kind of freedom.

However, I am also critical of what has happened today in Indian art because there still seems to be a great amount of exploitation by dealers — for instance, in grabbing up any kind of person who is Indian and who is painting and trying to make minor talents into major.

The art world is a wild place with all kinds of things happening. On the one hand, one of the best areas for American Indians to succeed in today is in the area of art, because there does seem to be a natural tendency for a very high esthetic sensitivity among Indian people. This is great, because art is one of the few areas that American Indians can excel in. But it's a double-edged sword because, especially in the Southwest, everyone is running all over everyone else trying to find the latest Indian talent, and they are getting people who really are just becoming formative in their own style.

Success can often be deadly to an artist if it comes too early. It often makes him just stop there, dead in his tracks, in a style that has become popular or saleable. In the last few years, a number of talents that were on the verge of becoming really fine talents have been stopped, mainly by success.

That's not just true of Indian artists. This is one of the pitfalls facing every artist. Some artists are never discovered, and they find this hard to believe. But success is one of the hardest things for anyone to handle. Success will always change your life.

Your full name is Fritz William Scholder the Fifth, and you have a son whom you have named Fritz William Scholder the Sixth. I am wondering what pressures, if any, you might be putting on your son.

First of all, he is the only one to carry on the family name, just as I was, and I felt almost obligated to do that.

At the same time I realized there probably would be pressure. I think any son or daughter of a noted person is under a great deal of pressure, just in that there's always a role model there that they have to live up to or at least react for or against.

My father was a regular father and in a way it was nice to have the same name. But often now people come up to my son and say, "Oh, you must be the artist."

How old is your son?

Twenty-one.

Does he paint?

No, he is studying to be a doctor.

Maybe if he becomes a very prominent physician, his reputation will even come to outweigh the paintings we see on the gallery walls.

We are looking forward to seeing the next avenue of approach for Fritz Scholder. Recently I enjoyed seeing a film of you at work in your studio, attacking that gigantic canvas with your brush, working with your paints in a small styrofoam cup.

Yes, I use styrofoam cups, catfood cans and all kinds of things.

One stroke you demonstrated was dipping your brush in the paint and letting the dots fall where they may. I have seen that in some of your other work. Is that a kind of trademark?

Not a trademark. Once in a while a special painting deserves that.

Ida Prokop Lee

Ida Prokop Lee's "Prairie Pictures" still hang in homes throughout the United States and a number of foreign countries. Ida created the colorful designs from North Dakota prairie weeds, grasses and pheasant feathers. The sale of these pictures, very popular especially in the 1950s, helped finance what was to become her life's work: a series of bronze busts of men and women representing each of the five North Dakota Indian tribes.

The busts were originally done in plaster; the collection was presented to the State Historical Society in 1957. Bronzes of the plaster busts, completed in 1981, now stand in the North Dakota Heritage Center in Bismarck.

We conducted our interview at Ida's home in Bismarck, properly cluttered surroundings with "Prairie Pictures" of various sizes adorning the walls and pieces of her sculpture filling tabletops and sections of the floor. A long table against the living room wall was topped with four of the magnificent bronzes, one of them a bust of Drags Wolf, a former chief of the Shell Creek Hoska clan from the Fort Berthold Reservation.

I ran my hand over the gorgeous headdress and touched the prominent nose and strong jaw on the deeply wrinkled, dignified face. The detail was amazing. Ida watched, standing a few feet away. She said nothing, but her smile told me of her pleasure that I admired her work.

As photographer Greg Mattern set up our camera and lights, the three of us talked casually about the weather, the coming spring and that summer's vacation plans. I had asked Ms. Lee to save any conversation about her work until the camera was rolling; it's always more immediate and fresher that way.

Suddenly our hostess let out a shrill cry and ran for the door leading to the back yard. At its entrance she grabbed a small air rifle set conveniently nearby. A squirrel had invaded her bird feeder. A couple well-placed shots, and the intruder headed for the upper limbs of the closest elm.

Greg and I watched the scene through the window. "What energy!" I thought. That's the essence of Ida Prokop Lee: talent and the energy to put it to creative use. And she's still going strong well into her eighth decade.

Ida, you are more than eighty years of age. They say it's not nice to tell a woman's age, but I think that you are very proud of the fact that at this ripe old age, you are still smack dab in the middle of one of your favorite art projects, your Indian series.

How did this Indian series become your life's work? When did you make your decision to devote so much of your time and energy to that single project?

When I was in my late thirties I started to work with moulage, the technique of making molds of plaster.

I had always been interested in three-dimensional art. My folks were photographers, and of course that's always flat. I wanted to create in the full three dimensions.

I worked with plaster a good deal at first, and then eventually with clay.

At the time my mother was developing the local doctor's X-rays for him in her darkroom. We lived in Lidgerwood at the time. I used to have a chance to borrow some of his magazines. One day I read a magazine article about a new waxy material we'd gotten after World War I from Germany. The German medical profession used it for research work, making casts even of the internal organs of the human body. I thought, "Ah, if they can use it on such delicate tissues, why couldn't I use it on the human face?"

You see, my folks being portrait photographers, I was always interested from the time I was a little girl in just what the human face would look like no matter what the material.

Those were tough days during the last part of the Dirty Thirties, so of course a dime was as big as a dollar. Nevertheless, I scratched together a couple of dollars and bought a couple of pounds. I experimented with it on a little girl, a neighbor and the daughter of a very dear friend of mine. And while the first one wasn't very good, the second showed some possibilities.

Tell us about this. What happened when you worked with the little girl?

The first experiment was not quite successful, but by the second one and the third one, I knew I really had something. So I decided to adapt it to something important.

I was a member of the Federation of Women's Clubs; that was in the years before we had a lot of radio and television, when the clubs were a way we could keep ourselves educated. I had high ideals, and I thought, "Well, as a clubwoman, what can I create with this process that we could all participate in and that would accomplish something worthwhile?"

I didn't know too much about the Indian people in those days, but I had a friend in Wahpeton, Esther Horn, who was also a club member. She was teaching at the Wahpeton Indian School. I laid the idea before her of getting a male and a female of each of the major tribes of our North Dakota Indians. I also originally included the children of the tribes, but I later abandoned that idea.

She said, "Oh, yes, it's a marvelous idea. You have no idea how important this could really be and I do encourage you to do it. If you want to, I will let you use some of the children in the classrooms for your models."

Esther also told me that she'd pose for me herself if I wanted her to. She claimed to be a descendant of Sakakawea on her mother's side, making her her great-great granddaughter. She said, "It always isn't accepted. I will fight for that for the rest of my life and never accomplish it — but I am, so if you want me to, I will pose for you."

So she was one of your first models?

My first adult model.

Now you're going to use the moulage process right on me for a demonstration.

We have a batch right here. You tell me this is almost like giving someone a facial. It's kind of a waxy substance.

Let me test a little of it on my own hand to see how warm it is.

OK, now you you're spreading it over the whole hand.

Yes, that's the basis of the whole sculpture. I cooked up this mess fresh just this last week, so it isn't really cured properly yet.

How do your subjects breathe when you are putting this on their faces?

Oh, I used to put straws in their nostrils, but I don't do that anymore. I have learned to control it, so I can just work it right up to the nostril and let them breath safely.

You're applying this waxy substance all over my hand. Now, if you were doing a full mask of me, Ida, how long would I have to sit for the application to dry before you would remove it?

Oh, probably a half hour. But you wouldn't mind. You probably would just go to sleep under it. This isn't the biggest problem, you see, because it's warm — a little more than body temperature is as hot as I dare put it on. And everybody is ready to go to sleep under it. It's almost like a beauty mask.

Were you the first to use this moulage process of taking a life mask from your subject?

As far as I know, yes, I pioneered in it. I had kind of an inferiority complex about using it for a long time.

Of course, I had done faces and bodies before, but just by hand with clay or with plaster, and I had quite a garden of statues of all kinds. We were too hard up to afford boughten statuary for my garden, so I made it. Those were rough years, as you know.

Now you told me that the first time you put one of these on and pulled it off, it collapsed in your hand. You had to devise backing of some kind.

You see, it's soft, and when I removed it from the face, it would flatten out. I had to make a plaster — I called it a mother mold because it holds it in place.

Now this is what I would do with you if I were seriously making a cast of your hand. I would make another mold over it. See, I would turn your palm like this. . .and then on the back of your hand also, and then I would separate it. I would end up with a complete model — perfect, much more perfect than any human hand could ever reproduce it.

Let's let this dry for a minute while you tell the story of taking, not a life mask, but a death mask of a legislator named Leif Twichell back in 1942.

He was Speaker of the House and very well known. He was an attorney from Fargo, highly respected and very beloved in the State Legislature.

They had a special legislative session in 1942. After it was over, he returned to Fargo and he passed away. Some of the state senators and representatives called me and asked me if I would make a statue of him. I said, "Well, I have never met Twichell in person." I had lobbied my bills through the Legislature to make my feather pictures legal, but I never worked with him, though he was a tremendous power in the House.

They suggested that I make the mask from his corpse. I had only tried that once on a little baby who'd died, so I told them I couldn't promise that I'd have much success.

You didn't do this until after his funeral, as I recall.

Yes, that's right. I said, "Go ahead and have the funeral services. Take him out to the cemetery if you wish, and then please bring him back to me and I will take him from there." So we did that. They took him out of the coffin and they laid him on a slab so I would have access to him.

I worked on his model all night. The plan was that I would make the positive cast as soon as I could the next morning and then call in some of his best friends, who could be the most severe critics, to find out if I got a good likeness of him or not. After all, the face changes in death. A lot depends on the mortician and what he does, and the condition of the body and so forth.

And so would I have a successful likeness, or wouldn't I? My method, I knew, was foolproof and much more accurate than the human hand could do. I not only got the anatomy but the details, even the pores of the skin. It was that much of a likeness.

You told me he had a little dent in one lip from carrying a cigar. . .

He was in inveterate smoker and he always chewed a cigar. It actually left a dent. You can go up to the Capitol building and you can feel it. The statue stands right at the entrance to the House of Representatives.

But when these critics came to view it, I said, "I don't want compliments; I want criticism because this has got to be good or I will destroy it at this point." I could have ruined my reputation; it was kind of early in my work at that time. So I wanted it to be very accurate, and they passed their OK on it.

One of the problems I had was that they didn't have a good photograph of him. particularly a side view. My biggest problem, then, was to get his posture right. Every man carries his head on his shoulders in his own particular way. I could only imagine that.

But when the bust was unveiled at a joint session of the House and the Senate I was asked to speak for a few minutes, and I asked the listeners to accept it as I had created it; if I hadn't gotten a perfect likeness in this case, to please realize that I worked on a corpse of a man that I had never met face to face. I told them I hoped that the statue would be a symbol of all the good laws that he had passed through the Legislature for the good of the people of North Dakota. And I never ever had a single criticism.

You speak of people being critical of your work or giving it criticism, constructive or whatever. You recently completed a bronze of Senator Milton Young which also stands in the Great Hall at the Capitol. It was criticized by a writer for a Minot Daily News as being a poor likeness or unflattering. How do you react to criticism of your work?

Somebody might criticize the work of a writer like him, too, you know. Perhaps I have that privilege.

He is entirely wrong in his opinion that it doesn't resemble Senator Young. I made the cast right off of his face and, despite all the criticism, it simply couldn't be otherwise.

Yes, he has large ears, as the writer pointed out. But I should have brought up a little model from the basement to show you. It's actually taken off of his ears — both ears — and everybody's ears aren't alike, you know. There's a great difference in ears. . .a lot of personality in people's ears.

And that writer said that Senator Young is humped over and the statue isn't. Well, with his disability, he is. I straightened him up a great deal more, but I didn't overdo it. After all, I did his face at his true age; he was eighty-two when I did him.

Unfortunately, he didn't have any wrinkles. I love wrinkles! They give character to a face. But you know very well, Boyd, that Senator Young has no wrinkles.

How was the Senator as a subject? Was he able to stay awake under this beautiful warm face pack?

That is one of the most difficult things to do! It's very, very relaxing. When I did my Lidgerwood doctor, he was accustomed to taking a nap at noon, and the only time he could give me was that period. He had been out delivering a baby all the night before. I had an awful time keeping him awake.

Senator Young, though, stayed awake just fine.

How did the senator feel about the bust? Did he like it?

He was very much pleased with it. So I was surprised to read that Minot critique, since I haven't heard any other criticism of if.

It's always just a matter of opinion.

Each of your pieces, Ida, has a story and a personality behind it. One of my favorites is the bronze of a man known as Strikes Two — Perry Ross, a former Marine. You took a moulage, or a face mask, from Perry at a very important time in his life, didn't you?

He had been in the Pacific Theatre of World War II. His eyes had been injured on maneuvers, and he was home on furlough between sessions of medical care.

My interpreter knew the Indian people very well. She said, "If you want a good male, Perry Ross is home today, but this is his last day. If you could stay overnight and if he will agree to pose for you, he would be a very good model." He was very well-built, of fine stature, and the Indian people are very proud of their warriors.

He agreed to pose for me, and I worked on him that evening and the next morning. I carved his eyes open even though he was blind. He went on to have surgery but became permanently blind.

He is still living up at Garrison, North Dakota. He is a very fine person, and we have developed a very warm relationship with his family.

He has never actually seen the piece, but has he ever had the chance to stand and run his hands over it so he can visualize it?

Well, Boyd, I didn't really realize he'd want to do that on the day when I presneted the whole Indian series of nine models to the State Historical Society way back in 1957. It was a very windy day. Two Coast Guard and Marine escorts led him up; he had a full Indian headdress on his head. He took it off and presented it to me.

I didn't realize that he hadn't been told that the fragile plaster model was present at that time. Now I am reproducing them in bronze, you see. But at that time he didn't have a chance to feel it, just to know that it was there.

The original went into a glass case at the museum, and nobody could touch it there. Plasters can be quite enduring, but the public can't get at them because they would maul and destroy them. That's why I am so glad now that we're going through this whole process of reproducing them in bronze so that people can feel them. That's an important aspect of sculpture.

So has your model had that chance to "see" it with his hands yet, now that it's cast in bronze?

Perry did finally have that chance a year ago last Easter. I invited him and his wife and daughters and sister for the first chance for him to feel the bronze casting.

And so he came and felt around the eyes and the ears and around the mouth and the insignia on his cap. He went on down, and he wasn't saying anything. We weren't saying much, just watching him. Then he came down to his left shoulder to the patch, as they call it.

For the sculpture, I raised it a little in relief. When Perry came to that, he started to feel it and counted the stars — one, two, three, four, five stars of the Southern Cross. Then he started to feel the hand with the torch, and he came to the number two on the torch itself. He felt of that, and he burst into tears. A grown man! He said, "The Second Division — that was my division." It was very touching.

Certainly Ida Prokop Lee will be remembered a long, long time for this Indian series and the bronzes that you have created. But if people somehow did not associate you with the bronze work, they surely would with something called "Prairie Pictures." You started creating them early on in your career; today those pictures hang not only in North Dakota, but all over the United States and a few foreign countries.

Many foreign countries, yes — and they originated here in North Dakota. The idea came from my lifelong love of hunting.

I used to go hunting with my dad and my brothers. My family settled in Richland County in 1881, when my dad was ten. In those days, the boys of the family generally had to supply the meat on the table, and he grew up loving it.

There were lots of prairie chickens when my brothers and sister and I were young, and so Dad figured that his daughters should learn to shoot as well as his sons. And I did. I became a real good shot. I think I had my first double-barreled shotgun when I was about eleven and shot it off in Lake Tewaukon, or "Skunk Lake" as we called it. It was muddy and the shots all went off at once. They sat me down in that mud good and solid.

You use the feathers from birds you'd shot. What other items went into these pictures?

I added native weeds and grasses of the prairies.

See, we grew up without much means and I didn't have art training. I didn't have materials to work with, except for things I found around my mother's studio. Both my father and mother loved nature, so all my work is founded on nature — and very intimately.

I found that not only were the feathers of pheasants so very beautiful; they don't fade in the sun. My pictures are very enduring. The weeds and grasses — oh, they have such beautiful textures! I learned to bleach them and then paint them with good oil paints that were as permanent as I could buy. I'd arrange the pictures, then, as a floral arrangement.

It was a hobby first of all. When did it become a business?

In the course of time, when I was going to start working on the Indian series, I had no means of supporting all the costs of that project. I was married at that time, but we were in reasonably modest circumstances, anyway. I didn't think my husband would have wanted to invest in work like that; and I was no longer working in the Post Office, where I'd spent thirteen years.

I decided to let art support art. I'd always thought that if I ever sold my pictures, it would kind of take the fun out of them by commercializing them. But I needed a way to support my art, so I looked around the many things that I worked with and I decided on the feather pictures. They were always so welcome as gifts to my friends, and they were not so very expensive to make. They were right at my doorstep, so to speak, not to mention out in the fields and ditches all around us.

The very early ones were made out of glass slides from our local theatre, the ones shown between reels. I melted the gelatin off of them and used those for the little ones.

The slightly larger ones were from my folks' photo studio. That was before roll film came into play; that was in the glass plate days of photography. I melted the gelatin off them, too, and used the glass.

Did you tell me that you used the sale of "Prairie Pictures" actually to finance the Indian project?

Oh, yes. Oh, yes, all the way through. They were a labor of love. The feather pictures became financially successful, quite a lucrative business. In fact, they developed much, much more that I ever dreamed they would.

People didn't realize, when they were buying my pictures in the one hundred stores that I supplied in the two Dakotas, that they were actually supporting this Indian project with those feathers.

So a lot of people have shared in this that never knew that they are a part of this Indian work. I produced over half a million of them.

You had a little difficulty at one time, didn't you, when the state determined that you were using feathers from a game bird in a commercial process?

"The sale or barter of any part thereof of a protected game bird, including the skin with the plumage thereon." Through all the years of my work in the Postal Service, I knew how to decode all the postal laws and regulations, so I knew there was no way of getting around that one!

Sure enough, one day I got a letter from the chief game warden that he had seized some of my pictures. Well, I'd known that this could happen. I was raising pheasants across the line in Minnesota by that time, and I had been investigating this law and trying to get a bill through the Legislature to change it. But I didn't know much about politicians and politics, and so I failed the first time I tried. I think it was about 1941. And so it would be two years before I would have another chance.

Minnesota had provided for pen-raising birds, so I hired a farm boy and his family to raise them in the pens for me. But just as soon as we brought those licensed, tagged pheasants across the state line into North Dakota, they were subject to North Dakota laws, so I was still in violation.

So, anyway, I got this letter from the chief game warden. I was called on the carpet! I came up to Bismarck. It was before we traveled very much, and I had never been that far from home at that time.

I met Governor John Moses first. I had written to Governor Moses because I felt that he had something to do with the appointment of the chief game warden who was after me; he was my enemy, of course. So I asked Governor Moses if he would pose for a bust for me, and very graciously he did. It turned out to be the start of a very beautiful friendship with him and his wife, and I stayed up at the mansion.

Wasn't it quite a coincidence that you happened to do a bust of the governor about the time your bill was being considered in the Legislature?

Yes, it was, wasn't it? Just before! I was laying the groundwork for it, of course. And it worked.

So you don't mind admitting to a little lobbying there with the governor?

No, no, I certainly did it.

Getting the bill through the Legislature was quite an experience. Quite an education, to lobby a bill like that. As soon as it was passed, the governor very graciously signed it immediately to put it into law.

So I didn't go to the state pen! They didn't have any quarters for women there anyway, I understood.

We are almost out of time. Unfortunately, I have tried to take some notes with the hand you were casting, and this moulage cracked.

Oh, it cracked for you! That's too bad.

My whole hand feels sleepy! I will tell you what to do — you keep this for posterity, and years from now someone will say, "Gee, that looks like the top of Boyd Christenson's hand." You don't have to do it in bronze. Maybe you can just keep it in the cookie jar.

I think that I might to that!

But I have to ask you one more question as an artist and a sculptor. You were telling me just before we sat down that you already have an idea of what you would like to have on your tombstone.

Well, yes. You know that I am teaching the man who is casting my bronzes many of the things that I have learned so he can carry on after me...although I expect to be around as long as Michelangelo, at least! Maybe one hundred. My grandmother lived to be ninety-eight, you know.

So I am going to take a lump of clay — I have worked a lot with clay and it's still my favorite medium — and I am going to have him make a model of me holding a lump of clay in my hands. I am going to name ti "From Clay to Posterity."

This will be a bust of you?

No, just my face and just my hands.

Your hands of clay.

Yes, that's all. That will be my memorial monument, the basis of it. That's how I want North Dakota to remember me.

The North and South Dakota people have been such wonderful people to work for and work with. It's been a pleasure and a privilege.

Cliff "Fido" Purpur

A couple of years ago Cliff Purpur stood in front of a packed house at the Grand Forks Civic Auditorium. His hands, rough and calloused from a lifetime as a carptenter, held the highest honor North Dakota can bestow on one of its native sons: the Rough Rider Award.

His eyes were filled with tears. "I love this state. I love the people. And I love all of you." The audience moved to its feet, and applause filled the hall. North Dakota loves Cliff Purpur, too.

I first met "Fido" during my student days at the University of North Dakota. The former National Hockey League star had returned to his old hometown to help establish a hockey program for UND's "Fighting Sioux." In addition to coaching the Sioux skaters, he worked by day as a carpenter; there were a lot of bills to be paid in a family that included six sons and two daughters.

When he wasn't pounding nails or tutoring young skaters, "Fido" would occasionally hold court at a neighborhood bar near the campus. We never tired of hearing his stories about the old days in the big league. As time passed the stories became familiar, but "Fido" would occasionally throw in a new wrinkle or a new character, and we were never sure how they were going to end.

He was usually dressed in a smudged felt hat, a flannel work shirt and a shapeless pair of trousers. A handshake with him was like gripping a piece of rough unsanded wood. Ah, the character in those hands! Usually two or three nails were blackened from a hammer's misdirected blow.

His speech was sprinkled with non sequiturs and slang and the occasional obscenity. It was not offensive. "Colorful" would be more correct. . .the communication of a common man.

But to describe Cliff Purpur as a common man would not do him justice. His loyalty and commitment to causes and people he believed in are truly uncommon. His adherence to *the work ethic is a model to his family and the many, many friends who know him well.*

"Fido" says it best himself: "No matter what you do in life, if you play the game square, you will always have friends, and they will admire you for it."

This man's name is synonymous with hockey, not only in North Dakota but wherever fans gather around the nation. Cliff, glad to see you.

Thanks a lot, Boyd. I'm glad to be here. We are almost like brothers.

As you said when I called you to do this interview, "If the two of us can't sit down and throw the bull for thirty minutes, then I have got us both wrong."

Well, we can throw 'er.

Cliff, let's start with the nickname "Fido." A lot of people probably don't even know that your first name is Cliff. How did the nickname come about?

A sportswriter in Minneapolis, Boyd, did a write-up in the "Minneapolis Journal." He wrote that I had a good night — you know, I got a couple of goals or whatever it was — and with one of them I was sliding on my stomach, you know, and I shot it right into the net on my stomach. So when he wrote about the game he said I was "busier on that ice than a springer in a field of pheasants."

But two days later here comes this other sportswriter and he dubbed me "Purp."

Purp...

Purp. Well, you've heard the people say that.

I remember one day in Chicago, Boyd — I remember so good. I went in to buy a pair of shoes. It wasn't very far from where I stayed. I come out of the store and I started to walk down the street, and I heard a kid yell, "Purp!" I thought he was calling me, like Louie Swenson always called me Purp. And I turned around and looked, and he was calling his dog. He didn't even know who I was.

A lot of young folks and even those of us in our forties probably know you best as the coach of the University of North Dakota hockey team, the man who actually started big-time hockey at UND. You were the man most responsible for getting a lot of little kids on skates in the city of Grand Forks and other cities around the state.

But there's another Fido who was a pro hockey star himself. Let's go way back to the 1930s. Cliff "Fido" Purpur was, at that time, the only American skater playing in the National Hockey League.

You went to St. Louis.

Right, the St. Louis Eagles. They had been the Ottawa Senators, and then they moved to St. Louis and became the Eagles. And that was the big news write-up in the papers: "Purpur from North Dakota."

So they made a big fuss out of the fact that you were a North Dakota boy.

Oh, yes. . .

And you would assume that if they are going to pick an American skater, he's going to be some big burly guy, six feet tall, two hundred twenty pounds — and you've told me that your heaviest weight ever in the National Hockey League was maybe about one hundred fifty.

I did get to a hundred fifty-seven once.

What was the National Hockey League like in those days? Let's start with the equipment. You obviously didn't have some of the safety equipment they have been using today.

Well, we never wore helmets, Boyd. They still don't wear them — a lot do, but not all of them — but none of us ever wore them back then. They figured you were yellow in them days if you put a helmet on.

What I would like to say to all of the kids is, "Be sure to wear a helmet to protect yourself." Like that Bill Masterton who played for Minnesota and was killed in hockey. If he would have had a helmet on, he probably would have never gotten hurt.

Now, in this day and age, when we think of professional athletes we also immediately think of huge salaries — a million dollars a year, five hundred thousand dollars a year. What were the salaries like for the players of the National Hockey League in 1934?

Well, we were paid on a twenty-week basis. And if you made $7,500 for those twenty weeks you were a good man.

Those were big bucks!

Oh, big! Well, I could have bought a new car, Boyd, in '36 for $675. But one of the owners of the club in St. Louis knew the fellow that ran the garage, so they got me my Ford for $575.

And I remember one night when I got my last check in St. Louis. I was going to catch the train home, but I waited for my last check — $700. I had the cab driver take me to the bank to cash it first. I never slept in that berth all night. I thought that if someone ever robbed me — well, that was a lot of money in those days.

As we said, you were the only American in the National Hockey League for awhile. How did the Canadians greet this little guy from Grand Forks, North Dakota? I'll bet you took your lumps for awhile until they found out who Cliff Purpur was.

I'll tell you the truth. . .I was a savage on that ice. And if I hadn't protected myself — boy, that would have never lasted. They would have run me right out. It's just like when I hit Joe Primeau in the training camp in the Toronto Maple Leafs' training camp.

Now, Joe Primeau was one of the big stars.

Oh, they were the two big stars, Joe Primeau and "Busher" Jackson. Then I caught them. I had that check — I could put them six, eight feet in the air without any sweat. I cut in on them quick, you know. Then once I took them out right at their knees, I could give then the old boost.

I shouldn't probably say this because too many kids will learn the habit.

But it was a clean check.

Oh, it never got a penalty, even. They tried to think up some policy — "We should kick him out of the hockey because he's too mean." And I weighed one hundred thirty-five pounds!

But about that time I hit Primeau: "Knuck" Irving had said to me, "We have got to beat the Toronto Maple Leafs, Fido."

I said, "You bet, we have to beat them!" Boy, a buck was a buck. I went up the hard way, you know. We were hungry.

Old "Busher" Jackson skated up and said to me — he swore at me, said he would kill me. The first time, I pretended I never even heard him. So pretty soon he skated at me again, and I said, "What did you say?"

He repeated the swearing words. He was going to kill me. I said, "You know what?" and he yelled real loud, "What?"

I said, "You're going next, you're going six or eight feet."

Boyd, he was the best friend I had from then on.

When we got in the dressing room — remember I'm the only American, and there are about fifty Canadians in there — "Knuck" Irving hollered, "I want all of you fellows to listen." He said, "I'd like to tell you that if they ever sent a two-hundred-pounder here from North Dakota, he'd wipe out this whole camp."

I said, "They don't have to send one. I'm here,"

I know there are so many pleasant memories you have had in this past year. You were named a recipient of the North Dakota Rough Rider Award, which is the highest honor this state can bestow. And I know you are also in the St. Louis Hall of Fame — with some pretty swift company, I might add.

Yes, I'm in about six halls of fame. The one in St. Louis isn't just for hockey. It was a hundred and five athletes of all sports who ever played for St. Louis. I was there, and there was like George Sisler, one of the greatest baseball players of all times, and Stan Musial. Stan Musial is a good friend of mine. When I was voted most valuable player in the league, George Sisler gave me one of the nicest jackets you ever want to lay your eyes on, a leather jacket.

You take Yogi Berra — he's a great friend of mine. When we went to Green Bay, we drove over to Milwaukee to watch a baseball game, too, so my boys said, "Dad, do you think Yogi could get us tickets?" I hadn't seen Yogi for over forty years, and the boys always kind of doubted me when I said I knew Yogi, you know. But I got the proof — in the "Hockey News" he said that I was his idol, and I've got the magazine.

When we got to Green Bay and saw the papers, we knew the tickets were all sold out all over. So I got on that phone and I got a hold of Minneapolis — I knew the Yanks were playing there. I called the baseball park there and the girl give me the address where the Yanks were staying. I called that place and I said, "I want to talk to Yogi Berra." About ten seconds later, he was on the phone. I said, "It's Fido Purpur."

We got to the game, though, and. . .no tickets. My boy Bob went to the window and asked if they had anything for Cliff Purpur. Nothing.

Then I told him, "Just a minute. Say, 'Fido Purpur.'" Yogi didn't even know what my first name was, I don't think. Tickets for Fido Purpur? Oh, yeah, they had tickets for Fido, but not for Cliff Purpur.

Then during the seventh inning stretch I jumped up and I went down to the usher. I said, "Where is the Yankees' dressing room?"

He said, "Just go down there, walk down that hall until you see that green door on the left," so I did. And I checked it; I asked the girl that was working in the concessions if that was the place and she said, "Right there, you're looking at the door."

So after the game was over, I said, "Come on, boys." We went down and knocked on the door, and the fellow said, "You can't come in this dressing room."

I said, "Tell Yogi Berra that Fido Purpur is here." He sure tuned down that boy in a hurry.

You know Scott, my boy, don't you? I got a kick after we visited with Yogi and we were walking down the hall to get to the car. Scott said, "I guess you really do know Yogi."

Now, Scott's your last son. How many sons have skated hockey?

All six of them. And the two girls were cheerleaders.

Have any of your sons made it in what we would call the major leagues of hockey?

Well, four of them played semi-pro, and they worked out with that St. Paul team and they were all scouted, but they were told they were too small.

You know, they want bigger men now. And I tell you — it's TV that has made it that way, that they want big men. And sometimes I think that people go to see fights, even. I know about three players who went to the University of North Dakota and were sent to a fighting school to learn boxing so they could play.

Now, what you're saying is interesting — in essence that instead of a player like yourself, one hundred thrity-five pounds, a good skater who can score goals and do all the things they can do in hockey, they are looking for the big burly guys who can muscle people.

They are thinking that way a lot more than they were back then, Boyd.

Is that the fans' fault? Are the fans asking for it?

You meet some fans who are getting tired of this fighting nowadays, you know. But then there are a lot of fans who I've heard tell me, "Boy, I sure like it when there's a good fight." But you don't need to be big. You see, I had a lot of fights and I was a little guy.

What is it about hockey people? Football games don't stop for a fight, basketball games don't stop for a fight. What's the answer?

Well, I can answer you there. I played football for Central High School in Grand Forks, so I know what's different. With hockey, it's that stick.

When you're hooking a guy with that stick, keeping at him, it gets awful tiresome. First thing you know, you turn around and you swing at him. You know, "Leave me alone!" That's what starts them.

It's different. There are a lot of players now that hold grudges all the time.

There were a lot of fights years ago, too, Boyd. Now, like me — I got three hundred stitches in my face, but I never got that from being hit with a fist. I skated so low to the ice, my nose was almost down on it. That's why they couldn't hit me, they couldn't get at me.

Let's get back to Scott, your last son. He's a pretty good hockey player, is he?

I'd say — one of the best.

Would you like to see him play in the National Hockey League? Is that kind of a dream, to see a son of Fido Purpur's in the NHL?

Yes, I would.

Do you think this one has a chance to do it?

I do.

You do — oh, yes. Wouldn't that be great to sit there in the stands and watch him, maybe for a North Stars game?

I would like to go back once more. See the old friends.

But you know, there are a lot of funny memories. The Sioux used to play in Denver in Colorado. They would complain, "Oh, I hate to go out to Denver — that high altitude. We get so short of breath."

So one time I said to them, "You don't have to worry. I got the medicine for when we get up in the mountains." All it was was Absorbine Jr., only I had it in a different bottle. So before the game started, I poured it in my hand and I smeared it under their noses — right under there. And you know, it does smell good, I smelled it myself.

Boy, they would skate back to the box — "Give me another shot" — so I would give them another smear. It was mind over matter.

Fido, I think a very important decision that you made was that you were all done playing in the National Hockey League, you made the big choice to go home to Grand Forks.

You had been a star, a "most valuable player." You had played for some winning teams. But one of the things you still wanted to do was to get the little kids on skates.

They told me, "If you stay, you don't ever have to work again."

I said, "No, I'm going back to North Dakota." I said, "If Minnesota can build hockey players, so can North Dakota." I had to go back somewhere to start it.

The game had to be built here, and it took some doing. That's why, when I had the Park Board kids' teams, I walked the streets raising money for banquets for them and gold hockey pins. I would take them to Devils Lake. I brought teams here to Fargo to build a game for the state.

And now it's spreading. I went to Wahpeton to give a speech last year because they are trying to get a rink now. And I would say that if we ever see rinks at Williston and Dickinson, then my dreams would have all come true.

Another dream that was fulfilled for you was when you brought big-time hockey to the University of North Dakota. Tell us about that first year, when they said, "OK, Fido, we want a hockey team."

What did they give you to work with?

I didn't get much of a salary, and "Red" Jarrett, the athletic director, said to me, "You can have the job, Cliff, but there is no scholarship money."

I said, "No scholarship money! How are you going to play the University of Michigan and all of those teams without scholarship money?"

He said, "I don't know."

I thought it over, and I finally took the job. So I went out and walked the streets. I walked the streets for a lot of week. I had to raise thousands of bucks so that I could get players in. You know, we didn't have enough American boys to go around.

One time on just six days' practice we played the University of Michigan, and here they had been on the ice a month. They had artificial ice. I knew then that I had to figure out a way to raise the money so we could get artificial ice to work on, too.

I got a price, and they wanted $17,000 for it for a down payment. The total bill would have been around $80,000 in those days for an artificial ice arena, but with the $17,000 down payment they'd get going on it.

It was July and I covered a lot of little towns asking for the money, you can believe it! But I raised the money so the university could get its artificial ice.

And then another big moment — I can even recall it, though it was before my time — was the year UND beat Michigan six to five. What year was that, Fido?

It was in the late 1940s.

That was the ushering-in. Here was the little University of North Dakota — no scholarships, rag-tag team, no place to pick up kids — suddenly beating a major, established college.

Of course, our team at that time was mostly American kids. There were the Johnson brothers, "Buzz" and "Prince." John Noah, the McKinnon brothers — Paul and Danny, Cal Marvin and George Dickenson. It's getting hard to remember all the names that far back.

Actually, they became legendary names associated with hockey in North Dakota.

Yes, it all just started rolling then.

The Noah name is still synonymous with hockey in North Dakota.

Oh, Johnny Noah has been a great friend. He was the one who nominated me for the state Rough Rider Award years ago, and pitched in after Jack Hagerty at the Grand Forks

Herald got a campaign going again last year. He put together a nomination with letters from all the college coaches, the governor, Yogi Berra, Joe Garagiola — all kinds of guys.

John has been a good friend for hockey, then?

Oh, gosh, he has built hockey here. He has done a lot for Fargo in hockey. I think it was John that really got Shanley High School going.

This is a great story and I know it's one of your favorites. When they built the brand new arena at the University of North Dakota some years ago and had the dedication, there were some special moments for you.

We were all at this banquet, Boyd, and these kids, all former players, were all hugging me and shaking my hand. They hadn't seen me for awhile. One kid had come all the way in from Toronto. I said to him, "Well, you came back to see the new rink, huh?"

He said, "No, I came back to see you. I want to thank you," he said. "Anything I get to be in my life I owe to you."

Then Bill Steenson said, "I wish you would have mentioned me on that, too."

So you see, no matter what you do in your life, Boyd, if you play the game square, you will always have friends and they will admire you for it.

What do you think of the style of hockey that they play now as opposed to the old style? Are they better skaters now?

Well, no. Howie Morenz still holds the world's record for carrying the puck around the rink. He's dead now, but I raced around the rink with him.

There were a lot of fast hockey players, but I would say that years ago you didn't open the game up. You only had to pass that puck in one zone, Boyd. That led to defensive hockey. If you got a one- or two-goal lead, you'd go into the shell and you could hold it. But now, the way they open it up, you can't hold a one-goal lead. Now you pass the puck almost the length of the rink. . .and get by with it.

You are not coaching anymore, are you? You are now sixty-nine years old.

I would not want to coach anymore.

I have coached Park Board teams. I have coached Central High School; I helped the eight of them who started hockey at Central High in 1940. When I came back it had died out, and the superintendent said to me, "We want to get hockey started again." So that's when Central High started to get back on the road.

One night we stopped in at a little bar in the city where the Amerks (a local amateur hockey team) were having a few beers. They said, "How about being our player-coach?"

I said, "No deal." They said they were drawing seventy-five people a game. I said, "Seventy-five people? Well, I wouldn't even care to put the skates on for that." But a few more beers led up to it, and finally I said, "OK, I will put the uniform on again."

Before we got done we were drawing more than three thousand people, as many as UND did. And that team went to the national tournament in Toledo. Oh, we had a good team, the Amerks. We even played the university.

Your Rough Rider Award was presented to you at a special dinner in Grand Forks a few months ago, and they officially installed your portrait in the hall in the Capitol in Bismarck. You have some pretty fast company: Roger Maris, Lawrence Welk, Anne Carlsen, Louis L'Amour, to name just a few of them. Tell us about your thoughts and feelings that day.

She was quite a deal, I'll tell you that!

They had notified me that we could all stay at the governor's mansion while we were in Bismarck. There were seventeen Purpurs who stayed there.

They asked me to be at the Capitol early, so we went through the new building, the Heritage Center, first. Then they had me talk to the press for awhile. They were covering me with lights and everything, you know, and — well, I can talk pretty quick, so they just let me go and pretty soon I was doing all the talking.

I can't imagine that.

I said to the sportswriters, "If you want to ask me any questions, ask them now," But they would not ask me any questions; they just said, "Let him go."

Governor Olson said he wanted me to give a big speech when they presented that scroll they give you. I told him I couldn't do it. Words are hard to find when you're standing there like that. So the governor unveiled that picture in front of my family and all of the people who were around there.

That scroll and everything — well, it was all just beautiful. And I thought, "Boy, this is really something!"

I want to end with a comment from a good friend of yours, John Noah, who said this one night at a banquet honoring you. He said, "If the world was filled with Fido Purpurs, everybody would get an honest day's work for a day's pay and there wouldn't be any wars."

I think I agree.